Dialogue

Proceedings of the
AIGA Design Educators Community
Conferences

SHIFT →

3–7 AUGUST 2020 * VIRTUAL SUMMIT
AIGA DEC STEERING COMMITTEE

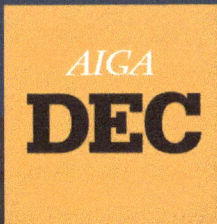

AIGA
DEC

I

SHIFT

Dialogue: Proceedings of the AIGA Design Educators Community Conferences

http://dialogue.aiga.org

Paperback ISBN: 978-1-60785-781-5
Open-access ISBN: 978-1-60785-782-2
DOI: https://doi.org/10.3998/mpub.12571098

Dialogue was conceived/designed by the AIGA DEC.

SHIFT Summer Summit Steering Committee

Ali Place, *University of Arkansas*

Alberto Rigau, *Estudio Interlínea*

Liese Zahabi, *University of New Hampshire*

AIGA Design Educators Community Steering Committee

David Hisaya Asari
California College of the Arts

Kareem Collie
The Claremont Colleges

Meaghan A. Dee
Virginia Tech

Gaby Hernández
University of Florida

Meena Khalili
University of South Carolina

Ali Place
University of Arkansas

Natacha Poggio
University of Houston
Downtown

Alberto Rigau
Estudio Interlínea

Kaleena Sales
Tennessee State University

Rebecca Tegtmeyer
Michigan State University

Brad Tober
Northeastern University

Kelly Walters
Parsons School of Design

Liese Zahabi
University of New Hampshire

Michigan Publishing

Jason Colman
Director,
Michigan Publishing Services

Carl Lavigne
Digital Publishing
Coordinator

AIGA Design Educators Community

MICHIGAN PUBLISHING
UNIVERSITY OF MICHIGAN LIBRARY

Dialogue is the ongoing series of fully open access proceedings of the conferences and national symposia of the AIGA Design Educators Committee.

Although each conference varies in theme, issues of Dialogue contain papers from DEC conferences which focus on topics that affect design education, research, and professional practice.

Michigan Publishing, the hub of scholarly publishing at the University of Michigan, publishes Dialogue on behalf of the AIGA DEC.

An Introduction

Shift. Shifting. Shifted. Various dictionaries define this word in ways that are both informative and quite poetic. A movement or beginning. An expedient necessitated by stress of circumstances; a forced measure. To make efforts, bestir oneself, try all means. A change of position or attitude.[1] To change or cause (something) to change to a different opinion, belief, etc. To change direction. To assume responsibility.[2] To put (something) aside and replace it by another or others; change or exchange.[3] Change is often thought of as frightening, frustrating, and unwelcome—but there is something about the specific connotations of the word "shift" that softens the impact, gives it a positive spin, even though these two words have very similar meanings. A shift feels more gradual, more attainable, friendlier, less abrupt. You can sense this in our everyday use of the word: The light shifted; she shifted in her seat; they shifted course; his thoughts began to shift.

As a computer keyboard (and typewriter) user of many years, I continue to be struck by the simple yet powerful capabilities of the SHIFT key. By holding it down in combination with other keys, you are able to reveal hidden characters, to transform visible characters, and to extend the potential of the keyboard itself. In this context, the word shift takes on additional meanings—allowing us to think about ways to transform, to expose, to reveal, to realign, to make our mark.

The mission of the AIGA Design Educators Community is to empower, support, and foster connection for *all* design educators. Our mission statement notes that as a group, "we seek to enhance the abilities of design educators and educational institutions to prepare future designers for excellence in design practice, design theory and design writing at the undergraduate and graduate levels while supporting the fundamental mission of AIGA." This is no small task—but it is crucial ongoing work that is absolutely worth doing. A part of this effort includes creating spaces that allow design educators to gather together, share ideas, work through challenges they face as educators and researchers, offer feedback and advice to each other, and to build community. The DEC was formed in 2004, and in the preceding years it has hosted numerous design education focused

"Nothing is so painful to the human mind as a great and sudden change." (Mary Wollstonecraft Shelley, *Frankenstein*)

"The only way to make sense out of change is to plunge into it, move with it and join the dance." (Alan Watts)

1 "shift, n." OED Online. December 2021. Oxford University Press.

2 "shift, v." Merriam-Webster Online. January 2022. Merriam-Webster Incorporated.

3 "shift, n. and v." Dictionary.com. January 2022. Dictionary.com, LLC.

conferences and symposiums—these events are more intimate than the large national conferences hosted by the AIGA, and offer a real opportunity for design educators in different regions of the US, at different stages of their academic careers, from different types of programs and schools to come together and learn from and connect with each other.

ABOUT THE SHIFT SUMMER SUMMIT

As the events of 2020 began to unfold in the US—beginning with murmurs of the COVID-19 virus in the first months of the year, leading to widespread uncertainty and confusion, and rising to a fever pitch in mid-March with a nearly nationwide pivot to remote teaching for higher education and K-12 alike—we were all desperately trying to figure out how to do even the mundane parts of our lives. How could we stay connected with our students? How should we teach our courses and finish out our semesters? How might we keep research agendas and design practices up and running when it felt like nothing would be normal ever again? Amidst this turmoil, in-person conferences and gatherings were postponed and cancelled, including the AIGA National Conference slated to be held in Pittsburgh, Pennsylvania that March (this event was postponed and reframed as a virtual conference held in November of 2020). Educators turned to social media to solicit help from equally bewildered and frustrated peers, but along with the physical lockdowns and social distancing, most of us felt a palpable sense of isolation, of having to go it alone.

The SHIFT Summer Summit was borne out of this shared sense of fear, uncertainty, and frustration. If we couldn't proceed with business as usual, what could we do instead, given our current situation and circumstances? Alberto Rigau (currently co-chair of the AIGA DEC Steering Committee) pitched the idea of hosting a virtual conference for the summer of 2020 during one of our steering committee meetings. He had helped to facilitate virtual conferences for other organizations and events, and thought that even as a small team, we could offer some kind of online event for our community as a way to gather together, share ideas, vent, commiserate, and most importantly, connect. As designers and educators, we know that we can do astounding things when we collaborate—we wanted to bring together, empower, and ignite our amazing and creative community.

Our team of three (Alberto Rigau, Ali Place, and myself)—with targeted assistance from the steering committee co-chairs Meaghan Dee and Meena Khalili, other DEC steering committee members, the AIGA DEI task force, and designers and design educators around the globe who generously served as volunteers, moderators, and panelists—built SHIFT during the summer months of 2020. We had sensed the need for such an event, but worried about the level of engagement the already exhausted and overwhelmed design community would be able to muster. Famously, one of us said, "If even 20 people come it will be worth the effort." The turnout far exceeded our expectations—we were blown away by how many design educators were willing and ready to come join us during those precious summer days—by the last day of SHIFT we had 828 participants signed into the summit Slack from all over the globe including 26 countries, and 40 different states here in the US, as well as the District of Columbia and Puerto Rico (and those numbers have continued to grow, as of this writing we have 1,581 members in the Slack). In those strange liminal and formidable circumstances, many of us were clearly seeking answers, ideas, resources, strategies, and most of all, the sense that we were not alone. That is why we wanted to organize this event, and that is what we hope you found (and continue to find) in this shared space.

5

As our team worked to create the SHIFT Summer Summit, our guiding principle was to bring together as many different voices and perspectives as possible, especially those that have been historically underrepresented in, or completely left out of, conversations around design education. Rather than elevate one or two established voices as keynote sessions, we decided every session topic should be explored by a group of panelists. We also decided live sessions should be structured within Zoom as meetings rather than as webinars—all attendees could see each other, could speak and share, and could be equally present within the discussions. We carved out spaces during each day for sessions we titled "mixers"—any attendee could come to these sessions to meet other educators and chat. Originally, we conceived of these in a "speed dating" format, where attendees would be shuffled into random breakout rooms and have just a few minutes to meet, and then be shuffled off to meet others. But during the week we quickly saw that what attendees wanted was more time to talk with each other, and sometimes even for everyone to stay in the same large room together. These mixers evolved organically over the course of SHIFT, responding to what the community needed the most, and the DEC has continued to host these sessions as part of our Virtual Events series.

It was important to the DEC steering committee to keep SHIFT free and open to *all* design educators and graduate students, which allowed us to build the enormous and diverse community of voices and perspectives in the shared Slack. This community includes design professionals with a teaching role at their workplace, design educators teaching at K-12 schools, designers teaching for organizations reaching out to specific groups of people, educators working in those tenuous adjunct and contingent roles, and

6

SHIFT

Fall 2020 Virtual Summit
schedule

→

monday
August

Conference kick off

A Community Welcome
Lee-Sean Huang
1:00PM

SHIFT WELCOME!
Introduction, Summit overview, what to expect during the week.
Liese Zahabi + Ali Place

AIGA Welcome
Bennie F. Johnson, Executive Director

DEC Welcome
A few words from the DEC Steering Committee Co-Chairs.
Meaghan Dee + Meena Khalili

DEI Welcome
A few words from DEI Taskforce representatives.
Carlos Estrada + Gaby Hernández

SHIFT Structure
Overview of Slack channels, some logistics, and an invitation to start the conversation.
Alberto Rigau

WELCOME MIXER
Our first 5-minute Mixers session, come meet some people!
1:30PM

AIGA **Design Educators Community** *the professional association for design*   **Diversity, Equity & Inclusion**

For links to all sessions

tuesday
August 4

Theme of the day:
TEACHING

DAILY INTRO VIDEO
Community responses.

MIXER
5-minute Mixers session focused on Teaching.
9:30AM EDT

Teaching the History of Graphic Design in the Contemporary Global Context
Roshanak Keyghobadi, Dori Griffin, Lisa Malone, Angela Riechers
11:00AM EDT

Human-Centered Design Education
Ali Place, Marty Maxwell-Lane, Kareem Collie, Jen White Johnson, Zachary Vernon, Victoria Shepherd, Jason Wilkins

Re-imagining the design classroom from the perspective of othered identities
George Garrastegui, Jessica Arana, Josh Halstad, Julio Martinez, Michele Washington

More is No More
Meena Khalili, Anne Stark Ditmeyer, (with Patricia Childers, David Habben)
ROUNDTABLE / 1:00PM EDT

Empowering students and building community through virtual critique methods
Rebecca Tegtmeyer, Kelly Walters (with Lisa Mercer, Khadijah Abdul Nabi)
ROUNDTABLE / 4:00PM EDT

MIXER
5-minute Mixers session focused on Teaching
5:45PM EDT

wednesday
August 5

Theme of the day:
RESEARCH

DAILY INTRO VIDEO
Community responses.

MIXER
5-minute Mixers: Research Edition (bring your 1-min elevator pitch)
9:30AM EDT

Design Research and Tenure & Promotion in the Age of Social Distancing
Liese Zahabi, Aaris Sherin, Anne Berry, Bernard Canniffe, Allison Puff

What Decolonial Design is NOT
Gabriela Hernández, Sadie Red Wing, Lesley-Ann Noel, Ahmed Ansari
PANEL CONVERSATION / 1:00PM EDT

Paths for Research
Meaghan Dee, Helen Armstrong (with Katie Krmarik)
ROUNDTABLE / 2:30PM EDT

Creating through Crisis: Time + Scale + Context
Noopur Agarwal, Jeannie Joshi, Danielle Foushée
ROUNDTABLE / 4:00PM EDT

MIXER
5-minute Mixers: Research Edition (bring your 1-min elevator pitch)
5:45PM EDT

thursday
August 6

Theme of the day:
COMMUNITY

DAILY INTRO VIDEO
Community responses.

MIXER
5-minute Mixers session focused on Community.
9:30AM EDT

Exploring Dualities: Design Educators Transition to Learning Designers
Alana Hawkins, Sudebi Thakurata
11:30AM EDT

Overload: A Talk on Mental Health and Design Education
Kaleena Sales, Shannon Doronio, David Walker, Ebonee Lyle

Developing a collective accord for community engagement in design education
Rich Hollant (with Kathy Mueller, Pouya Jahanshahi, Zoe Chatfield)
ROUNDTABLE / 1:00PM EDT

Who Gets to Teach?
Jacinda Walker, Paul Nini, Mari Mater O'Neill, Aisha Densmore-Bey
PANEL CONVERSATION / 2:30PM EDT

From local to global
Natacha Poggio (with Cynthia Lawson Jaramillo, Alejandra Zambrano)
ROUNDTABLE / 4:00PM EDT

MIXER
5-minute Mixers session focused on Community.
5:45PM EDT

friday
August 7

Conference Closing

Bitter Sweet: The End
Wrapping up the week
1:00PM EDT

Summit Recap
Lee-Sean Huang and Community Members

Call for Submissions
Liese Zahabi

Virtual Happy Hour
2:30PM EDT

= ASL Interpreter Present
L = Live Session
O = View On Your Own Time

e summit Slack, for more information go to educators.aiga.org/shift-2020

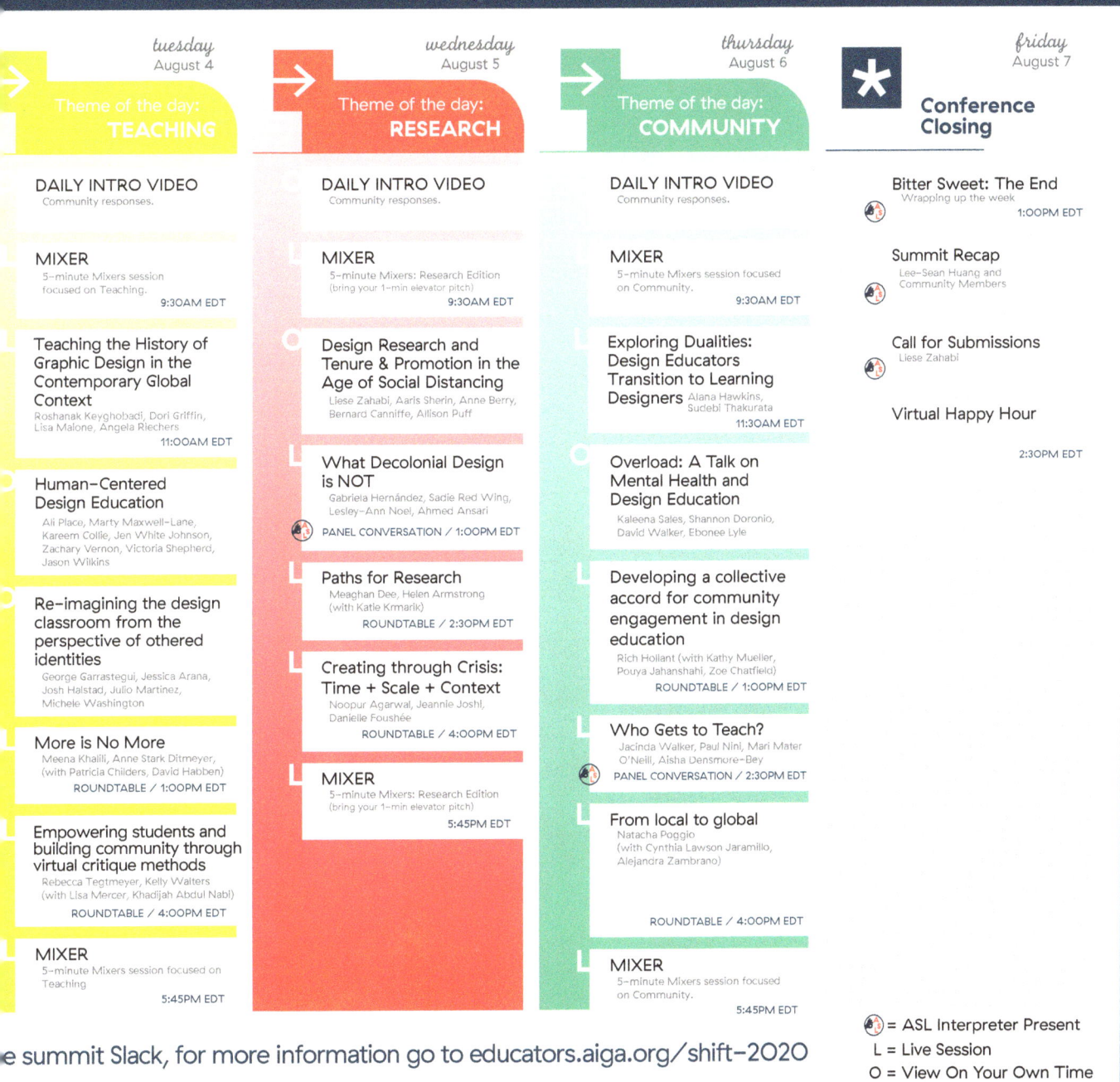

Figure 01: Full schedule for the SHIFT Summer Summit, which took place August 3–7, 2020.

design faculty in all levels of higher education. We were also thrilled to see how focusing on open access allowed for a more global audience. The community that formed during SHIFT has continued to talk, share, and connect in the Slack, and if you haven't joined us there, we hope you will do so soon!

The SHIFT summit was organized around the themes of Teaching, Research, and Community. We wanted to highlight often overlooked perspectives and facilitate meaningful dialogue around these three central aspects of design education, creating space for the community to grapple with the sweeping changes happening within design education. During the summer of 2020 design educators were trying to figure out how to teach remotely or while wearing masks; were navigating issues of tenure and promotion amidst a global pandemic; were attempting to conduct (or defer) research with altered time constraints, funding, and social distancing requirements; and many were starting or continuing the critical work of making our classrooms, pedagogies, and design communities more diverse, equitable, and inclusive. Our goal was to create an event that would leave participants with some new ideas, practical resources, provocative questions, new friends and colleagues, and hopefully, some hope.

Sessions throughout the week included a mix of pre-recorded sessions, live panels, and live roundtable discussions. Bracketed with an opening and closing session, over the course of the three core days of the summit we hosted four pre-recorded panel sessions, three pre-recorded intro videos that included submissions from the community, seven live mixer sessions (and a happy hour on the final day), and ten live panel or roundtable sessions. Through the dedication and extraordinary efforts of those working behind the scenes (namely, Alberto Rigau), we were able to post recordings of all of our sessions (except for the mixers which were unrecorded) to our public YouTube page within 24 hours, furthering the reach and accessibility of these important conversations. You can see the full event schedule in Figure 01, and can access a playlist of all the SHIFT recordings at https://www.youtube.com/c/AIGADesignEducatorsCommunity/playlists.

We built SHIFT for *you*, for our vibrant community of design educators—but one of the most gratifying and satisfying aspects of SHIFT was that this event was in part built *by* you. It was constructed as a framework that could be shaped as it took place—flavored by the dialogue that happened in the moment during the live sessions, by the vibrant conversations taking place on the Slack, influenced by the work of our tireless volunteers and moderators, and constructed through the insights and expertise of our speakers and panelists. And these conversations continue to happen, as the shift we are all still making together continues on.

MOVING BEYOND SHIFT

As we think about all the sweeping changes taking place right now, it is easy to focus on all the ways that things aren't the same, aren't normal, aren't the way we would like them to be. But, this new reality gives us the chance to not only create new ways of doing things (because we must) but to also rethink all our previous approaches and question their validity (because we should.) This is true for the ways we teach, make and design, conduct research, serve our campuses and communities, practice self-care, consider our stances on inclusivity and diversity and accessibility, and how we show up for each other.

Conferences serve the community in many ways: to share and disseminate information, to present research and ideas and get feedback from a body of peers, to swap ideas and tips. But most importantly, conferences allow us to connect, to gather together, to be present in space with others. Most of us have likely attended physical conferences in the past, and many of them have been wonderful, perhaps even life-changing. The implications of the COVID-19 pandemic have meant that we cannot currently replicate those conferences of the past. However, maybe that's not altogether a bad thing. What happens to our ability to connect when we are no longer bound by geography or funding? How much more accessible and inclusive can we make our gatherings when we completely rethink how a conference is meant to be structured or framed? I believe these are incredibly positive advances in how academic conferences and gatherings are structured, and I'm so excited to see how these events continue to evolve.

When I look across the past two years, at the community built in our Slack, and the community we built together during SHIFT, I am hopeful that we can break down the hierarchies of those conferences of old, remove the elevation of singular (and often the same) voices, empower different voices to come to the forefront and share, and really put our trust in our community to help us build—from the bottom up—a new way of approaching design education, not just in the U.S., not just for academics at Research 1 universities, not just for full time faculty, but for all of us. There is so much to learn, so much to share, and so much to build. Most importantly, WE NEED YOUR HELP—yes you, the one reading these words in this moment—and I fervently hope you will continue this journey with us.

FINALLY, PROCEEDING TO THE PROCEEDINGS

The SHIFT Summer Summit was a completely different kind of conference for the DEC. Part of this difference meant that we did not solicit proposals or abstracts from educators to construct the content of the event. Instead, we used the summit as a catalyst for conversations, as a place to incubate ideas, and framed these proceedings as a way to more formally publish and disseminate thoughts and research sparked by the content of SHIFT. The contents of this document showcase research, pedagogy, and opinions springing *from* and *about* the SHIFT Summer Summit, rather than a documentation of the content of the summit itself.

We received submissions from educators all around the world, and conducted a rigorous double-blind peer review to select the papers and essays included here (a double-blind peer review means that reviewers did not know the identity of the authors they were reviewing, and authors do not know the identity of the generous peer reviewers who assessed their papers and gave feedback.) Found in these proceedings are design educators directly discussing their experiences connected to the COVID-19 pandemic, a much-needed manifesto focused on the idea of a "Human-Centered Design Education," pieces examining aspects of design history, work examining ideas connected to diversity and inclusion, guidance for design educators wishing to write for scholarly journals, and much more. The papers found in these proceedings suggests the breadth and depth of the work those in our community are doing, and I hope you enjoy hearing from these diverse perspectives as much as I have.

This is a unique moment in time, and the energy within this community is both palpable and incredibly exciting. We need to do our best not to squander it! Please stay engaged, please reach out with questions or for help, please share your ideas and resources, and join us as we continue to build our future, right underneath our feet, as we move forward.

Liese Zahabi

Assistant Professor of Design,
University of New Hampshire,
New Hampshire, USA

SHIFT

3–7 AUGUST 2020 ✳ VIRTUAL SUMMIT

AIGA DEC STEERING COMMITTEE

10

Short Papers

SHIFT →

AR — moving a print class into an augmented reality

DANNELL MACILWRAITH
Assistant Professor,
Kutztown University,
Kutztown, Pennsilvania, USA

Keywords
augmented reality, print design,
design education, online education,
poster design, social media

The pandemic has seen much of education move online and some of it is likely not to move back. For instance, many of us are now very comfortable with technologies such as Zoom for both classes and meetings. Among the myriad other ways in which COVID has accelerated existing trends is the plummeting consumption of all kinds of print media. Newspaper companies have been hit hard: among the six publicly traded newspaper companies studied for a Pew Research Center report, advertising revenue in the second quarter of 2020 fell by a median of 42% over the last year (Barthel, Matsa, & Worden, 2020). I had first-hand experience of both these phenomena when, in the midst of lockdown, I was asked to teach a poster design class to seniors at a state college in the Northeast.

Pre-COVID, the eight-week course centered on the creation of two print projects: a poster advertising a Smithsonian museum exhibit and a gig poster for a band of each students' choosing. But how could I teach a poster design class without printing anything and without the class being able to experience their work displayed in a public space? The doors to our school's print center had been closed since March 2020 and few people were spending their time strolling around outside admiring posters.

I began researching how to translate the elements of my poster class into an online modality.

Poster design is one of the most popular classes we offer but what would students expect of such a class during a pandemic? Some objectives of the syllabus would simply not be possible, such as "experiment[ing] with paper stock and printing processes" and, in a virtual setting, we couldn't experience the posters in the same way; touching them was of course impossible, for example. The class had to evolve and it went in the direction of digital posters, social media advertising campaigns, Zoom backgrounds, and—most excitingly— augmented reality (AR).

AR is technology that allows the viewer to look at the world mediated through a mobile device, overlaying information and virtual objects onto the real world in real time. It takes the existing environment and adds to it (Marr, 2018). AR is now available to everyone, thanks to the phones in each of our pockets. There are many useful applications for AR: you can try on clothes virtually without going to a store; you can navigate your way through a busy airport; and you can alter your face in all manner of ways with the latest filters on Instagram and Snapchat.

The next step was researching various interesting ways in which print and AR had already been shown to work together. How could the concept of "poster design" incorporate this new technology while still resulting in something resembling a poster? Answers were to be found in products such as the Toy RC Car *(https://play. google.com/store/apps/details?id=com.CendaGames.RemoteCar)*, where users print out paper tracks on which a remote-control car adventure takes place; in Holotats *(https://holotoyz.com/)*, which are stick-on "tattoos" that you print out and then use AR to help them come to life; and in coloring books which become animated when

14

viewed through a phone screen. Our new goal would be to do something similar: to create an AR experience.

We began with students developing concepts for each of their projects that we felt were distinct enough that the viewer would not be distracted by the interactive elements that we would be adding later. Students produced thumbnails (half-size compositions) of their ideas using traditional media (pencil and marker pen). We discussed the experimentation involved in the making of an original artwork, copyright, storytelling, and typographic hierarchy. This part of the course was not too different from any other year.

Then we entered new territory. I had revised the course in three important ways: by keeping a focus on strong communication design, by finding appropriate and compelling ways to display the final work, and by creating an experience with usable AR software. Once the students' initial sketches had been produced, as a class we discussed ways to transform them into AR experiences. How could we expand on the ideas in the poster to create additional backgrounds and objects? What demographic would benefit most from the virtual experience? How can virtual interaction be a substitute for 'real world' posters? We considered the benefits of virtual versus in-person. The students had strong options both ways—some saw the potential of digital experiences but many were still eager to both create and display something firmly in the real world.

Next, we discussed the means of creating AR environments. There are several popular applications which do this but, in a graphics and print class, many of the students were intimidated by the technology and coding involved. I briefly introduced Spark AR, Adobe Aero, Brio, and UnitedAR as applications commonly used in the AR world. Each piece of software is suited to different needs and difficulty levels.

I wanted to minimize technical barriers and avoid additional costs so I chose to focus the class on Spark AR, created by Facebook, which is an augmented reality platform for Mac and Windows that allows you to create AR effects for mobile cameras relatively easily. Anyone can create and publish their own Spark AR effects for Instagram. This free software can transform

a traditional poster campaign into an immersive AR experience.

For those seeking an alternative to Spark AR, I would recommend Aero, part of the Adobe Creative Cloud, which allows the viewer to interact with the AR environment. Layers of graphics created in Photoshop create a sensation of depth in the AR image seen through an iPad or iPhone. Adobe Aero adds a whole new dimension to the way designers tell stories. For more advanced creators, Brio is great for creating 3D objects for both virtual reality (VR) and AR environments. For example, if you wanted to add a hat into your AR environment, first you would create a 3D prototype in Brio. Next you would add the 3D object to Spark AR. The hat may now be used as an Instagram filter.

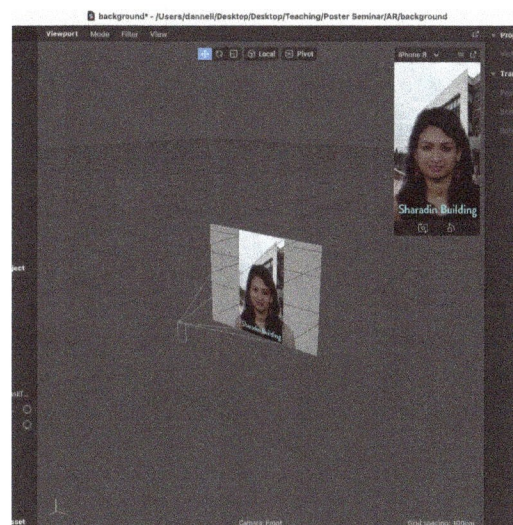

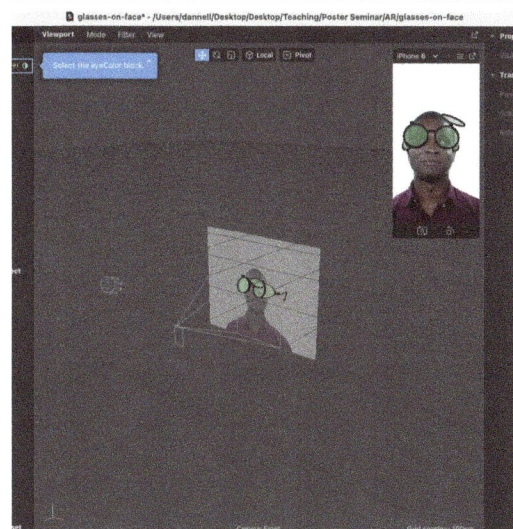

Screenshots of SPARK AR, created by Facebook, an intuitive, free AR application.

15

AR poster *"Outbreak: Epidemics In a Connected World"* saw germs floating around the viewer. Left, digital version of poster.

AR poster, for the Smithsonian "Magnificent Obsessions", utilized the background and foreground to create depth, while butterflies circled the viewers.

AR poster allowed viewers to interact with a mask by moving around inside the AR environment.

By creating AR posters that users could interact with, students were able to question their concept of poster design. The poster *"Outbreak: Epidemics In a Connected World"* saw germs floating around the viewer; the *"American Female Inventors"* exhibit asked *"Which Female Inventor Are You?"* and the answer came as images cycled above your head and finally landed on one; another project allowed viewers to interact with a mask by moving around inside the AR environment.

The course provided students with plenty of new experiences and gave us all a new conception of what poster design could mean. With the inability to travel or print, the new syllabus was a necessary—and welcome—change. Haptic feedback and audio elements included in some of the designs really captured people's imaginations. The students hadn't realized exactly how intuitive and easy AR development could be, or what interesting new opportunities would arise for students, giving them the chance to collaborate in new ways. Furthermore, these technologies may end up playing an important part in some students' work lives. As a professor, the process of transforming a traditional class into something much more expansive made me think again about the benefits that AR and similar technologies could offer other courses. Truly a worthwhile experiment!

CITATIONS:

Barthel, M., Matsa, K. E., & Worden, K. (2020, October 29). Coronavirus-Driven Downturn Hits Newspapers Hard as TV News Thrives. Retrieved June 29, 2021, from Pew Research Center's Journalism Project website: https://www.journalism.org/2020/10/29/coronavirus-driven-downturn-hits-newspapers-hard-as-tv-news-thrives/#f-nref-83725-3

Marr, B. (2018, July 30). 9 Powerful Real-World Applications Of Augmented Reality (AR) Today. Retrieved June 29, 2021, from Forbes website: https://www.forbes.com/sites/bernardmarr/2018/07/30/9-powerful-real-world-applications-of-augmented-reality-ar-today/?sh=7d0a72f52fe9

Designing Interventions for Multi-modal Classrooms: Using Machine Learning to advance Human-Centered Design Education

KYUHA SHIM
Associate Professor,
Carnegie Mellon University,
Pittsburgh, Pennsylvania, USA

Keywords
artificial intelligence, design education,
human-centered design, interaction
design, machine learning, multimodal
interaction

EXECUTIVE SUMMARY

The sudden shift in education to online learning in response to COVID-19 has revealed several challenges to using video-based platforms. This illustrative case study explores a few of the most prominent issues of virtual platforms, such as screen fatigue and a decrease in social interaction, through design interventions that enable multimodal interactions powered by AI.

BACKGROUND

The events of 2020 required design educators to shift modalities, from in-person to largely remote. Teaching on virtual video call-based platforms has significantly reduced the quality and quantity of social interactions I had on a day-to-day basis with my students and the chitter-chatter among the students has been replaced by the silence of various chat rooms. Comparing the same courses I have taught over the years, it has taken more effort to create a lively environment and encourage active engagement by the students on virtual platforms. The need to augment engagement on virtual platforms, particularly, requires great effort, as was discussed during the AIGA DEC SHIFT Summer Summit in 2020 (AIGA Design Educators Community, 2020). At the same time, the solutions should not solely be governed by these virtual platforms. In 2017 the AIGA Design Educators Community published *AIGA Designer 2025: Why Design Education Should Pay Attention to Trends*, which discussed ways that systems built with Artificial Intelligence (AI) would yield diverse ways of participation and format of engagements (AIGA & Google Design, 2019). AI is a computational system that performs tasks related to human intelligence such as learning, problem-solving and pattern recognition. Additionally, the respondents of the AIGA Design Census 2019 speculated that AI / Machine Learning (ML) is the technology that will most likely be our future (AIGA Design Educators Community, 2017). ML is an approach to implement AI by training a model that can recognize patterns. AI / ML has enabled designers to deal with complex problems that are difficult to be resolved using conventional programmatic methods, and has greatly impacted the way designers work. In the context of envisioning a way to utilize AI / ML to diversify engagement, how might we improve the virtual environments for design education?

STRATEGY

In my course 'Computational Design Thinking', offered during the Fall semester of 2020 at Carnegie Mellon University, I assigned a 6-week project that asked students to design an interactive system that presents an intervention in the context of online design education. Students (12 Junior- and Senior-level undergraduate and 3 graduate students) were encouraged to explore the most prominent pain points and opportunities they experienced in video-based communication platforms. Each team of students investigated situations in which there are newfound difficulties in communication due to the pandemic. The project brief was to strategize and develop concepts by utilizing machine intelligence, and to identify novel ways to introduce appropriate interventions through multi-sensory experiences.

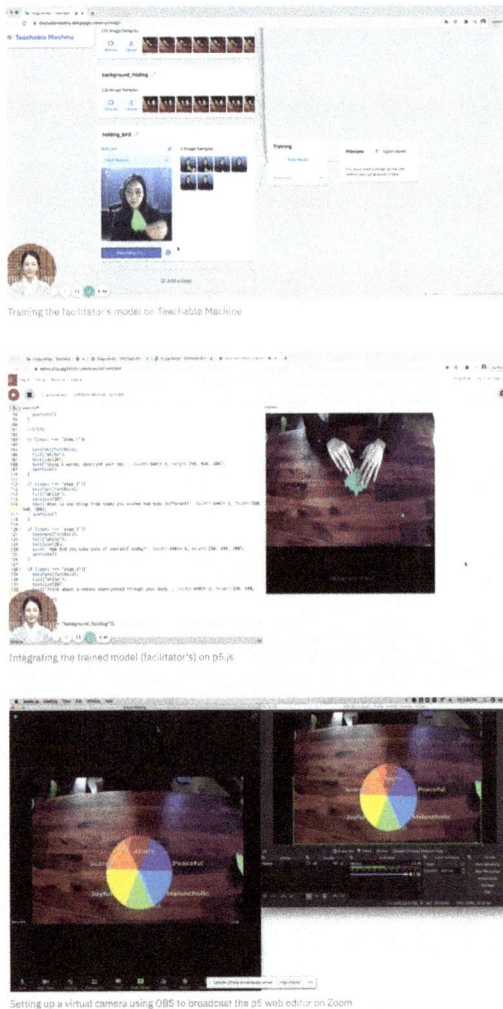

Figure 1: Screenshots taken by Taery Kim in the process of training, coding, streaming systems. 2020. Taery Kim. Top: Training an ML model in Teachable Machine. Middle: Connecting the ML model with p5.js. Bottom: Using OBS to broadcast p5 screen using the ML model (http://www.kimtaery.com/works/work-b)

DESIGN APPROACH

The project required that students use Google's Teachable Machine, a web-based tool for creating machine learning models that can recognize images, sounds, and gestures. Without directly working with code, students were able to easily train classifying models by defining the classes (categories of data) and generating the data by either uploading or capturing audio/video using a microphone or webcam. The trained models were imported into p5.js editor, a web-based Javascript library and creative coding platform, to build an interactive system that converts human behaviors (input) into dynamic visual outputs. For example, waving a hand might be captured and used as a trigger to activate a dynamic visual response on HTML Canvas. Finally, to live stream the interactions in a video-based call (Zoom), students utilized a broadcast software, Open Broadcasting System (OBS), to display what's drawn on the canvas on Zoom. As a supplementary resource, the students utilized The Coding Train's video tutorials by Daniel Shiffman to learn how to integrate Teachable Machine and Zoom using p5.js and OBS. While a typical process for prototyping interactions through programming might require designers to specify all the cases within their systems using conditional statements (e.g., if/else), using an ML model required an entirely different process. The students were required to design their own logic to use the trained models as smart sensors that convert behavior into a few classes that they determined appropriate.

PROJECT OUTCOME

The first student group investigated ways to improve social communication between participants of Zoom for collaborative image-making through gamified interactions. Their final outcome was a multi-person game that occurs on the Zoom platform and enables multiple participants to interact with each other in real-time. Their approach was to use the platform to build a social system for creative expressions, rather than resolving a discrete existing problem with the interface. The game encourages collaborators to talk to each other while working on their image-making challenges on-screen. In addition to standard device inputs (i.e., keyboard, mouse) for controlling the position of their pixel brush, the game enabled the participants to draw with an image captured on their webcam and utilize particular sounds (i.e., clapping hands, paper rustling) to control the resolution of the images. As a concept that provides a playful experience for remote participants, their project successfully delivered a way to leverage physical objects in the participants' own surroundings for collaborative making. The widely used collaboration platforms such as Figma or Miro have offered highly convenient and practical

18

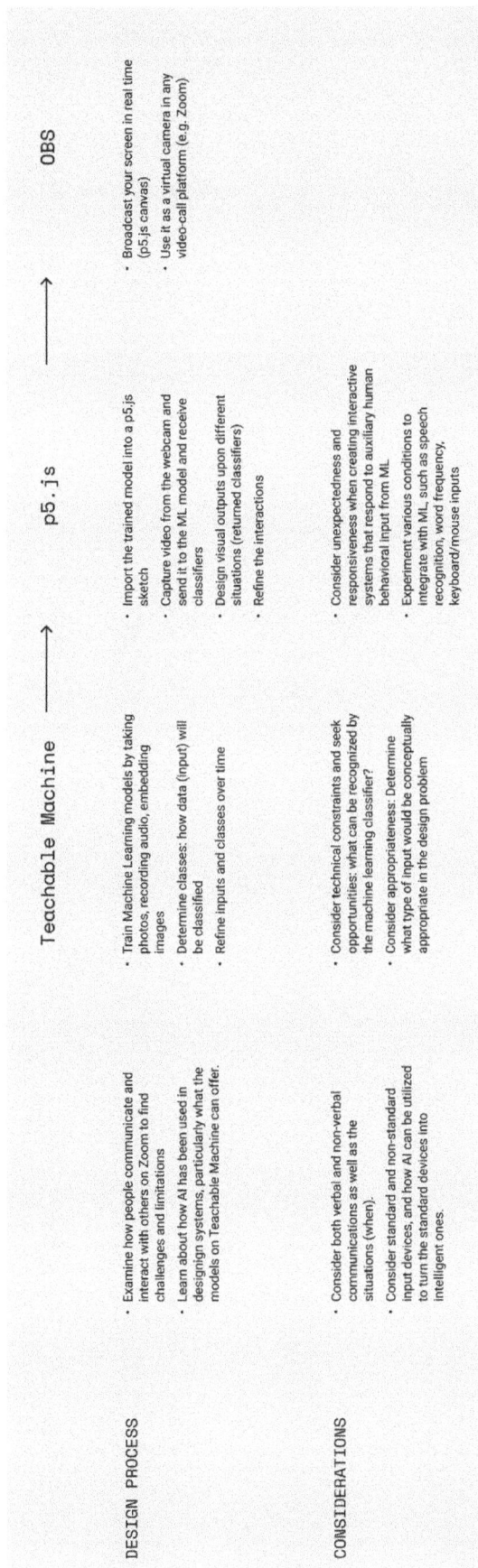

	Teachable Machine →	p5.js →	OBS
DESIGN PROCESS	• Train Machine Learning models by taking photos, recording audio, embedding images • Determine classes: how data (input) will be classified • Refine inputs and classes over time	• Import the trained model into a p5.js sketch • Capture video from the webcam and send it to the ML model and receive classifiers • Design visual outputs upon different situations (returned classifiers) • Refine the interactions	• Broadcast your screen in real time (p5.js canvas) • Use it as a virtual camera in any video-call platform (e.g. Zoom)
CONSIDERATIONS	• Examine how people communicate and interact with others on Zoom to find challenges and limitations • Learn about how AI has been used in designign systems, particularly what the models on Teachable Machine can offer. • Consider both verbal and non-verbal communications as well as the situations (when). • Consider standard and non-standard input devices, and how AI can be utilized to turn the standard devices into intelligent ones.	• Consider technical constraints and seek opportunities: what can be recognized by the machine learning classifier? • Consider appropriateness: Determine what type of input would be conceptually appropriate in the design problem • Consider unexpectedness and responsiveness when creating interactive systems that respond to auxiliary human behavioral input from ML • Experiment various conditions to integrate with ML, such as speech recognition, word frequency, keyboard/mouse inputs	

Figure 2: Design Process and Consideration. 2021. Kyuha Shim.`

environments; however, this project offers a game-like board where they continuously negotiate and work collaboratively to draw things using a webcam and microphone. In the context of virtual classrooms, this project showed a great possibility for using AI as a multimodal collaboration medium for creative hands-on activities.

The second group investigated language and etiquette on Zoom and conceived responsive avatars that augment participation. The main component of the outcome was a responsive flower avatar that reflects participants' behaviors on the platform. The flower grows as the participants speak and perform certain actions, such as raising their hands or giving a thumbs up. During the live demonstration of the project, it was surprising to see that the avatars were highly visible even when there were more than 30 people in the Zoom room. By bringing in an element that is continuously responsive to a participant's behavior, the project has encouraged behavior that will increase human-to-human engagement in virtual interactions. The group aimed to actively foster conversations and to encourage the participants to turn on their cameras and contribute to discussions. As an exemplary design system using machine intelligence to recognize human speech, face, and gestures, the concept provided a playful way to improve the limited existing emoji features on Zoom.

The third group investigated issues of fatigue, isolation, and lack of social communication in virtual classrooms and designed an activity-based workshop. The outcome was a set of tools for facilitating and/or participating in a communal paper-folding and journaling exercise. In the specific context of university classrooms, this system focuses on two user groups. First, the instructors, who are provided with a tool for leading a therapeutic group workshop and track the progress of the participants. Second, the students of the workshop, who have the tools to aid self-reflection and connection with the instructor and their classmates. This group utilized two image-based machine learning models and built a system comprising of an emotions key, a set of self-reflection questions, visual feedback, and audio response. The facilitator demonstrates the steps of origami (paper-folding) and triggers a self-reflection

19

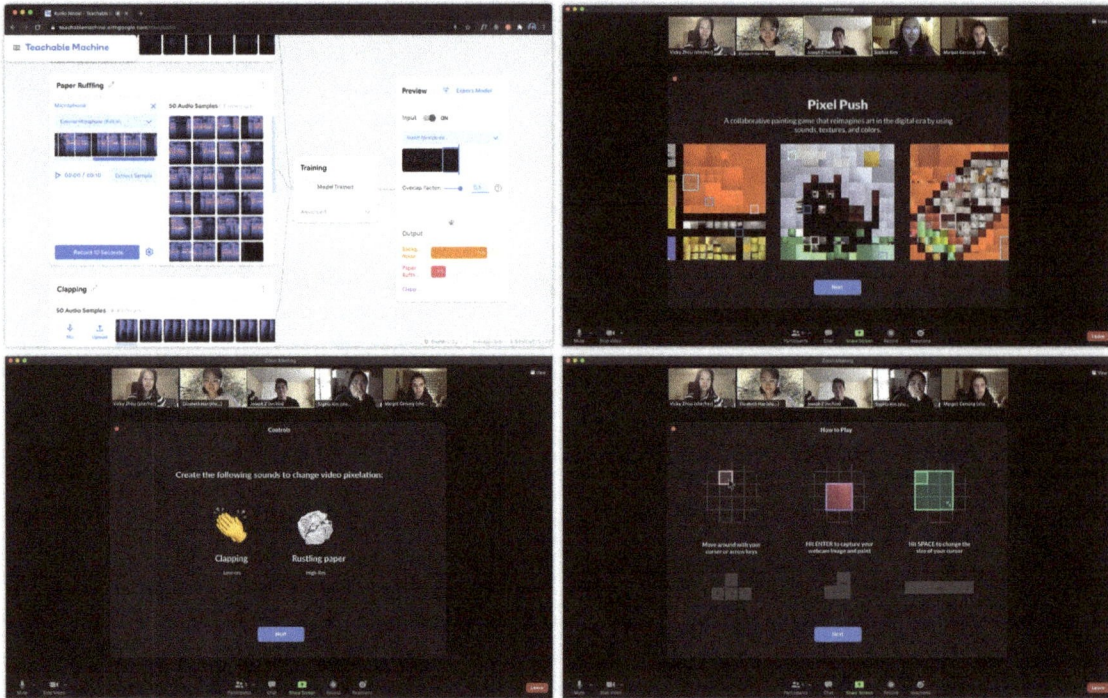

Figure 3: Pixel Push. 2020. Margot Gersing, Elizabeth Han, Sophia Kim, Joseph Zhang, and Vicky Zhou
(https://josephz.notion.site/Pixel-Push-48910c3a971747b0b6fc3f31572b9984)

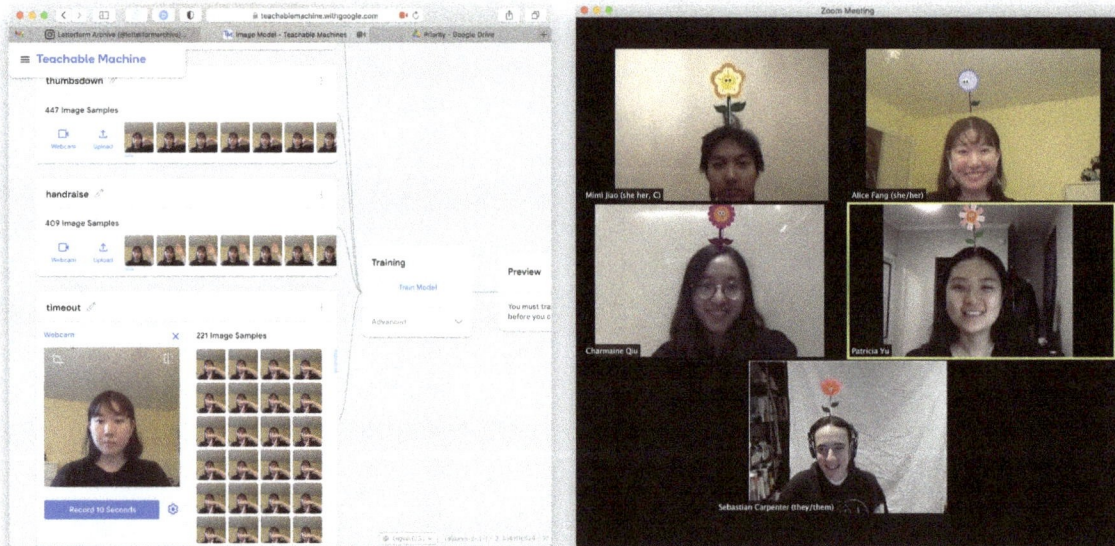

Figure 4: Conversation Gardens. 2020. Sebastian Carpenter, Alice Fang, Mimi Jiao, Charmaine Qiu, and Patricia Yu
(http://alicefang.me/Conversation-Garden)

question that appears on-screen at each step. The participants fold and journal their responses on their folded origami-in-progress, and trigger a visual response that indicates they are complete. A key component of the workshop is an emotions checkpoint, at the beginning, mid-way, and end of the workshop. The participants are asked to use the provided emotions key and hold up a piece of colored paper that best represents their current emotions. The system generated visual responses comprised of various cut-out shapes of flowers and animals that appear and disappear on their individual screens. Through the workshop, the group aimed to enable an

Figure 5: Unfolding. 2020. Yuran Ding, Jenna Kim, Taery Kim, Nandini Nair, and Stefania La Vattiata (http://www.kimtaery.com/works/work-b)

emotions-aware, caring environment on Zoom, in which the instructors and students would be encouraged to augment emotional literacy in their communications.

CONCLUSION
(INCLUDING CHALLENGES, EFFECTIVENESS)

The shift in design education towards remote settings has yielded a decrease in participation and engagement, as well as a decrease in social and emotional connections. As such, the shift has accelerated both the imaginations and implementations of AI in the context of design education, as well as in its mode of delivery. Through this course project, the students explored ways to utilize machine learning to devise new interactive systems that are multi-sensory, multi-modal, and encourage new forms of interaction on existing video-chatting platforms. It is significant that the use of AI has informed the students to be more attentive to how we communicate in different circumstances. What the takeaways from these projects and students revealed is that there is great optimism for devising systems that rely on human behavior, rather than systems that require humans to conform their behavior to fit specific input requirements of hardware devices. All the groups addressed challenges we face in virtual social communication and presented different ideas for improvement, through a multi-person game, responsive avatars, and a therapeutic workshop that relied on participants' actions using speech, face, and gestures. A key significance of utilizing AI in design systems is that we do not always have to be bound to existing algorithms or scope of technologies. Perhaps a lasting impact of this shift will be encouraging more design educators to demystify AI, use it in their classrooms, and encourage students to take a human-centered approach by utilizing AI to build systems that serve more natural, humanly interactions.

REFERENCES

AIGA Design Educators Community. (2020, August 4). Panel: Human-centered design education | SHIFT Virtual Summit 2020 [Video]. Youtube. https://www.youtube.com/watch?v=fA-vsL6C99GY

AIGA., & Google Design. (2019). Design Census 2019: Understanding the state of design and the people who make it. https://designcensus.org/data/2019DesignCensus.pdf

AIGA Educators. (2017, August 21). AIGA Designer 2025: Why Design Education Should Pay Attention to Trends. AIGA Design Educators Community. http://educators.aiga.org/wp-content/uploads/2017/08/DESIGNER-2025-SUMMARY.pdf

SHORT PAPER

Human-Centered Design Education: A Manifesto

ALI PLACE
Assistant Professor of Graphic Design
University of Arkansas
Fayetteville, Arkansas, USA

MARTY MAXWELL LANE
Associate Professor of Graphic Design
University of Arkansas
Fayetteville, Arkansas, USA

Keywords
design education, human-centered
design, equity, empathy, access,
agency, care

The calamitous events of 2020 forced design educators to shift many things—from the way we teach our classes, to the role we play in our students' lives. These events also forced us to reckon with many problems that have existed in design education yet have gone largely overlooked, such as inequities in the student experience, access to tools and technology, access to support, and the impact on mental health and wellbeing. With these concerns front-of-mind, we convened a panel of design educators from a wide variety of higher education institutions, including Hispanic-serving institutions (HSIs), historically Black colleges and universities (HBCUs) and community colleges. The aim of "Human-Centered Design Education" at the AIGA Design Educators Community SHIFT Virtual Summit was to explore the ways in which design education can and must shift in order to serve the student as a whole person. The discussion was framed through the lens of human-centered design, an approach to design research that we often teach in our classrooms.

Human-centered design meets people where they're at. It is a process that takes into consideration their pain points, their limitations and their unique needs. It fosters agency and collaboration, and employs empathy and reduced hierarchy in order to create positive outcomes for the user. This panel posed an important question: As design educators, are we practicing what we preach? Or do we perpetuate a one-size-fits-all experience that centers dominant narratives and marginalizes others? This question becomes particularly important in the context of remote learning, a modality that many were forced to adopt during the pandemic. In a meta use of the term, the panelists' conversation explored the ways in which the principles of human-centered design can guide the ways we approach teaching design by centering the needs of students. Education during a pandemic continues to be marked by uncertainty and challenging circumstances, so how can we ensure that our students have safe, supported, and successful learning experiences?

What the pandemic revealed to us as a society was how precarious so many people's lives have always been—teetering on the edge of financial, social, and emotional collapse for so long that one calamitous event sent millions of lives into crisis. Our students were no exception. They lost jobs, lost housing, lost access to social support, lost access to tools like computer labs, took on new caregiving duties, encountered new mental health challenges or had existing ones amplified by increased stress and anxiety. Through this panel discussion, we hoped to emphasize and normalize two plain facts: that students are whole beings, and design professors are not experts in all things. By framing our teaching around these small revelations, a model for design education emerges that centers students' experiences and engenders a culture of curiosity and care. When they leave our classrooms, we don't just want them to be great designers—we want them to be great and ethical humans. We want to prepare them to address the social, cultural, and political systems they will live and operate within.

22

What follows is a manifesto inspired by the key topics addressed in the panel discussion. This manifesto is intended to prompt a re-imagining of the teacher's role and a re-envisioning of the design classroom centered around the notion of students' and educators' humanity as assets, not liabilities. This manifesto is for all design educators who are exhausted by the status quo; who reject the capitalist interests in the design discipline; who reject the over-policing of students in the classroom; who believe that higher education can serve students better and are committed to changing the way things have always been done. And, of course, this manifesto is for our students.

WE WILL PRIORITIZE ACCESS.

We acknowledge the myriad barriers to success that students may face in design education, including technical, financial, and cultural. We commit to designing courses and programs that address and mitigate these barriers by ensuring students have access to the tools, support, and mentorship they need in order to succeed. We commit to cultivating an equitable learning experience for all students and to directly addressing inequities faced by vulnerable students. We reject allegiance to industry standard software, and instead commit to promoting acts of making that center outcomes and are software- and tool-agnostic. We commit to creating and promoting a diversity of access points to design education, especially outside of 4-year programs.

WE WILL FOSTER AGENCY.

We commit to facilitating a classroom environment in which students are agents of their own experiences, outcomes and assessments. We acknowledge that what students have to offer as designers is valuable, not in spite of, but rather because of who they are outside the classroom. We will value the knowledge that students bring to their education, including their culture and life experiences, and we will provide opportunities for them to apply their knowledge to design. We reject the notion of what the discipline has traditionally regarded as "good design," and instead will cultivate in students an ability to think critically through the lens of their own perspective and worldview. We will give students the opportunity to participate in their own assessment and take ownership of their contributions to the classroom. We commit to holding space for students to collectively develop their own studio community and culture that authentically represents them.

WE WILL EMPLOY EMPATHY
AS A TEACHING TOOL.

We commit to creating course structures and program policies that do not seek to punish or disparage vulnerable students. We reject discriminatory practices that further harm marginalized students, such as inflexible attendance policies, in favor of inclusive practices, such as engagement policies. We commit to accommodating all learners through our course materials and tools, understanding that designing for the most vulnerable students will improve the experiences of all students. We acknowledge that "vulnerability" encapsulates a dynamic set of experiences and circumstances, and vulnerabilities can also be superpowers. We commit to fostering an environment where students can show up fully as themselves and be successful.

WE WILL INTERROGATE AND DISMANTLE
TRADITIONAL HIERARCHIES.

We reject the master/apprentice teaching model and embrace a reduced hierarchy in the classroom that empowers and cultivates students' own experiences, skills, interests and abilities. We commit to dismantling power structures in the classroom that marginalize students from underrepresented backgrounds. We embrace vulnerability and honesty as means to build trust. We commit to building relationships with our students based on collaboration and mutual accountability. We recognize that it is our responsibility, as people in positions of power, to call out and dismantle inequitable power structures in education.

WE WILL PROMOTE A CULTURE OF CARE.

We reject the pervasive "hustle culture," or "culture of suffering," in design education. We embrace a culture built on reciprocity and collaboration. We embrace our role as more than professors, serving as co-explorers, co-collaborators, role models and mentors to students. We commit to fostering trust in our

23

relationships with students so that they feel comfortable communicating with us about their needs. We commit to fostering safe spaces where students feel seen, heard, and valued. We commit to seeking and celebrating joy and curiosity in our studios. We recognize the studio environment as a community that thrives on shared accountability and collective success.

WE WILL HOLD SPACE FOR WHAT WE DO NOT KNOW AND WHAT OTHERS HAVE ALWAYS KNOWN.

We reject the notion of the "professor as expert" and embrace a continuous mindset of lifelong learning. We will hold space for students to be the experts in their own experiences, cultures and narratives, while de-centering ourselves as instructors. We will model traits such as curiosity and humility as designers and as citizens. We commit to broadening the canon of design by centering the voices of marginalized people whose knowledge and skills have been lost, denigrated, or devalued for so long. We embrace alternative forms of knowing, making, and doing. We embrace the current climate in education as an opportunity for collective liberation and tearing down silos.

WE WILL CARE FOR OURSELVES SO THAT WE MAY CARE FOR OTHERS.

We recognize that we are better educators when we not only give, but also receive. We commit to advocating for ourselves in academic spaces, and making our needs known. We will establish healthy boundaries with our students and our work, particularly in the remote teaching environment, by protecting our time and our space. We will model self-respect and healthy working behaviors for our students. We embrace a culture in which educators support each other, and reject the culture of zero-sum competition. We insist that there is liberation in cultivating a shared success.

24

We share this manifesto with gratitude for the conversation with the panelists: Kareem Collie, Jen White Johnson, Victoria Shepard, Zachary Vernon and Jason Wilkins. We acknowledge the responsibility that we have as educators to re-examine our role in problematic systems and commit to pushing our discipline towards a more just, empathetic, and inclusive model.

Professor, Partner, Parent, Practitioner: Making Room to Evolve in Academia

MEENA KHALILI

Assistant Professor,
University of South Carolina,
Columbia, South Carolina, USA

Keywords
parenting, COVID-19, diversity,
equity, inclusion, design education,
professional practice

ABSTRACT

As the framework of design education and design practice at large continues to push against historical, societal, and cultural norms toward equity, actively supporting a broader scope of humanity through diversity and accessibility, there is a need for a reconsideration of refractory systems which have long influenced parenting in academia. Normalization of parenting alongside work as pedagogical researchers and practitioners would power careers in academia to be increasingly accessible and consequently more diverse. This paper discusses this issue as it relates to impacts of COVID-19 in the United States and aims to add to the current discourse surrounding the topic.

INTRODUCTION

Sometime in March 2020, after another consecutive day of working from home full time with our toddler, my partner and I carved out 90 minutes to prop our eyes open with toothpicks and watch a documentary on American conceptual artist, Mark Dion. Mere minutes into the film Dion made this comment about his son:

> Fairfield is my almost two-year-old son, who is here to make sure that none of the goals I have of this project can actually be achieved. He is a 30-inch tornado in my life...His presence here in some way helps take me out of my own methodology. I know how things should proceed and Fairfield, with his demand of time and energy, throws a wrench into that.[1]

Exhausted without childcare and amid the hairpin turn from classroom to Zoom room, Dion's opening spoke to us in our new never-ending Groundhog Day of parenting, practicing, and teaching with all its difficulty and beauty. We were at the precipice of what would become a globally shared journey: COVID-19 not only turned our respective classrooms upside down, but also threw a wrench into our creative practices and research agendas. Additionally, we had just accepted new jobs, relocated 500 miles from our friends and family, and had a fresh toddler.

The circumstances painted above are not wholly unique.[2] The complexities of parenting while in academia are documented in myriad publications. Many of these publications take a gendered approach focusing on female academics and how they might navigate motherhood in academia, or in turn, how they might navigate academia in motherhood. Yet in March 2020 working parents across the globe watched schools shut down while education on the whole began support of at-home virtual learning.[3] Daycares closed[4] and as pre-K to graduate school shifted online[5] parents and caregivers across gender and occupation—even C-level executives—suddenly found themselves working from home full time while parenting.[6]

CONSIDERATIONS

Flexible and empathetic approaches to teaching can support learners in reciprocal ways, which in turn can have an effect on

25

student success and retention.[7] Data from the Collaborative on Academic Careers in Higher Education (COACHE) Faculty Job Satisfaction Survey indicate 53 percent of faculty members are parents or caregivers: About 16 percent are parents to an infant, toddler or preschool child and one-third are parents to a school-aged child. Sixteen percent have a college-aged child and 12 percent are caregivers for a dependent adult.[8] The impacts of these statistics find their way into the classroom. For instance, two separate occasions went viral in 2019 at Georgia Gwinnett College and Morehouse College respectively. In both instances professors at these colleges exhibited unique compassion as they held babies for their students while continuing to lecture so those students without childcare could be free to take notes.[9]

The COVID-19 pandemic has altered our collective view of global and economic culture. Healthcare, childcare, school, and employment took center stage on the 24-hour news cycle and took personal, emotional, and physical tolls on all of us.[10] Amid these concurrent extremes, discussions of misconception, bias, and discrimination were happening at louder volumes, all while a wide range of working parents struggled to find care and deliver virtual instruction.

We are long past the time to openly discuss the needs of parents, soon-to-be parents, and caregivers in academia. Now is the time for academic parents to openly and clearly articulate their unique perspectives. In what ways can institutions best support academic parent performance? How can we generate the momentum needed to propel this conversation forward?

SURVEY

Any discussion best suited to further the dialogue surrounding this topic must include a diverse range of perspectives from those who have experience parenting and working in academia, and must reconsider the role of gender in parenting and caregiving. Additionally, to provide more thorough information on this topic it is imperative to obtain input from various types of instructors teaching in a diverse range of colleges and universities to include traditional and non-traditional institutions, minority serving institutions, teaching focused

universities, community colleges, and research-focused universities.

A survey around this topic was developed to aid in this research. It considered the influence parenting in academia may have on partnership and career. This survey collected responses from 30 anonymous parents in academia over the course of 36 hours in November 2020. Regarding limitations: to keep engagement, the survey was capped at 15 questions, three of which were long answer (see *Appendix A* for the complete list of 15 questions). Specific questions about ability, gender, and age were not asked in this brief survey, although respondents often suggested that information in their written long answers. It was posted to social media channels frequented by design and art educators, requesting participation from parents and caregivers in academia, and garnered the following results.

The lion's share of respondents had more than six years' experience, but 16% are still within their first six years in academia *(see: Figure 1)*. Most are *full*

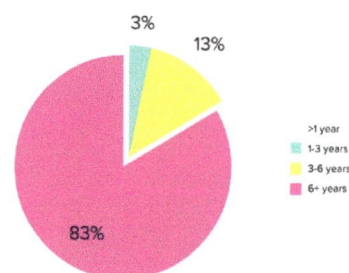

Figure 1: *How long have you been teaching in academia?*

time tenured or *tenure track*. The survey allowed for participants to write in their titles, which accounted for *adjunct, professor of practice,* and *administrators.* While most results came from research-focused four-year colleges or universities, there was a healthy amount of response at teaching-focused four-year colleges or universities, Historically Black Colleges and Universities, and community colleges.

Thirty percent of survey respondents indicated having a partner or marriage with someone who teaches full time in academia. Those respondents in a marriage or partnership with someone who teaches full time in academia were all working at 4-year colleges or universities.

Figure 2: *On a scale of 0 to 10, what impact has the response to virtual, hybrid, or HyFlex instruction due to COVID-19 had on your teaching?'*

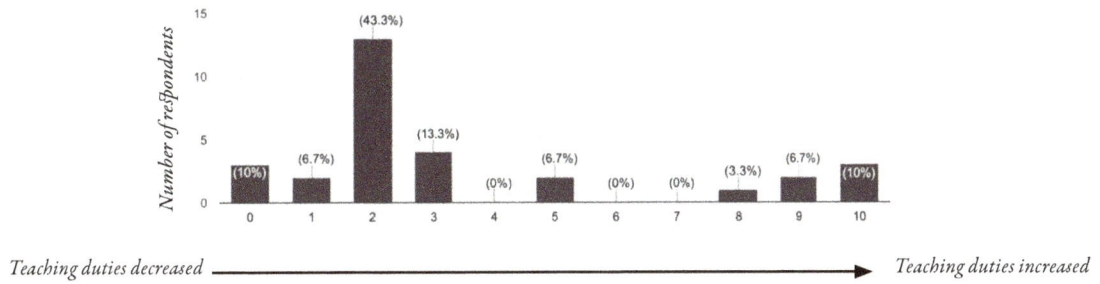

Teaching duties decreased ➝ Teaching duties increased

Figure 3: *On a scale of 0 to 10, what impact has the response to virtual, hybrid, or HyFlex instruction due to COVID-19 had on your research?*

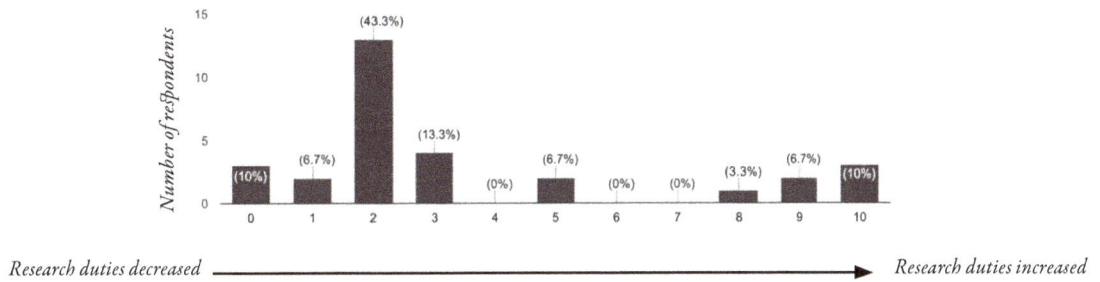

Research duties decreased ➝ Research duties increased

Figure 4: *On a scale of 0 to 10, what impact has the response to virtual, hybrid, or HyFlex instruction due to COVID-19 had on your service?*

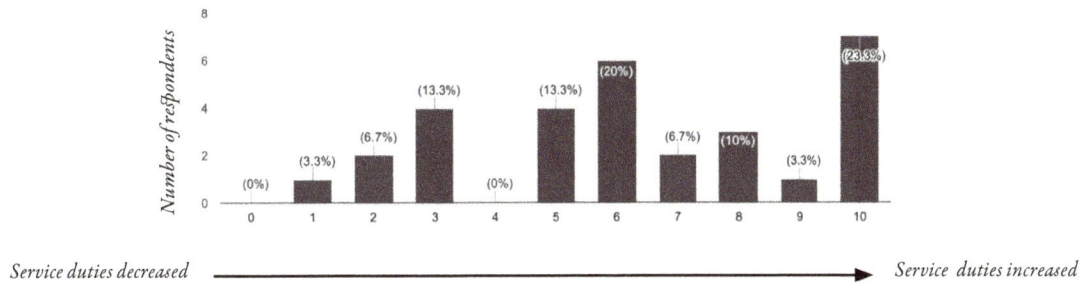

Service duties decreased ➝ Service duties increased

This survey also asked respondents about impacts from the sudden response to virtual, hybrid, or hyflex instruction due to COVID-19 (*see: Figures 2-4*). Most saw an increase in their duties related to teaching. Surprisingly, few saw a decrease in their research as most respondents reported little impact on their research due to COVID-19. But service jumped for most, hitting the higher range of the scale.

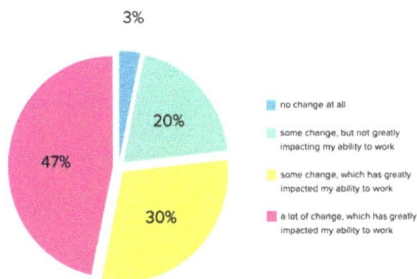

Figure 5: *Please indicate the level of change in your duties as a caregiver and/or parent.*

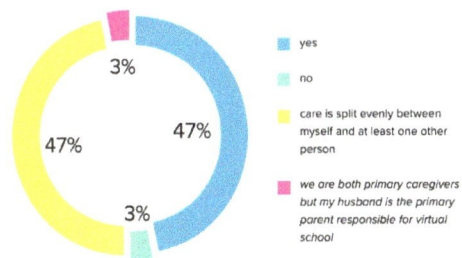

Figure 6: *Are you a primary caregiver and/or parent?.*

When asked to indicate the level of change in duties as a caregiver and/or parent since COVID-19, 77% of respondents indicated some change to a lot of change greatly impacting ability to work (*see: Figure 5*). Almost half of respondents indicated themselves the primary caregiver or parent, or that care is split evenly between themselves and at least one other person (*see: Figure 6*).

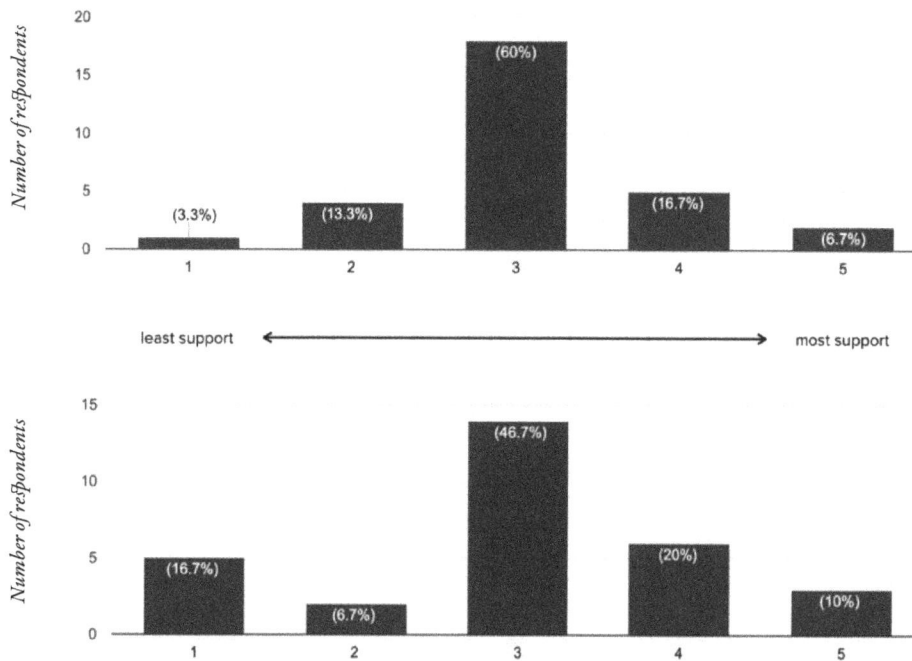

least support ⟵————————————⟶ most support

Respondents were given the option to rate their work environment based on its support for caregivers and/or parents both prior to COVID-19 and *since* COVID-19. This survey found that most considered their institution to be *neither supportive nor unsupportive*. However, those who were ambivalent about support prior to the pandemic indicated a more extreme response post-pandemic declaring either *more support than before* or *less support than ever*. The final three survey questions were open to length and specific responses have been selected for this paper.

Question: Has the decision to parent while in academia influenced your partnership?

Responses:

> There's not enough time in the day to be a good parent, partner, and professor.
> Because we're all working from home now, our work is much more visible to each other. This creates an illusion of focusing more on your job than your family. At what point does being a workaholic mean you value your job over your family? It's a constant struggle: I love my job and I love my family, but I'm tired of being judged for working so hard, yet also judged for having a family.
> At my previous teaching job (at a community college) faculty received a 40% discount to quality on-campus daycare, which was a facilitating factor in having a child. Moving to my current 4-year institution with no support for childcare and lower salary meant we were not able to pay off debts. This affected our financial decisions, retirement and security greatly.
> Yes. It has literally put my career on hold. I am pausing my tenure clock.
> I am in academia so I make less money; because I make less money, I can't afford full-time childcare; because I'm the primary parent, I don't pursue research or creative practice where I don't know how much time it's going to take per week/month/etc. Everything has to fit, so it's hard or impossible to take big risks with time.

28

> I'm not making much work or writing much. I'm barely keeping my head above water in terms of teaching. Service and committee appointments have increased, and I usually juggle those with my kids in zoom school. At my school no consideration is given to working parents on an administrative basis except to say, "Oh, it must be hard." My partner is very supportive, but her research is exceptionally demanding, and our lives weren't constructed to have two kids at home and work full time.

> Yes, I waited until I had tenure to start a family. In my post tenure review, I was told I was not doing enough research. But having a baby isn't something you can mention in your post tenure review file.

> We operate our household on a day-to-day basis, fulfill our wide variety of parental roles/responsibilities (and simply love our children and each other), while still meeting the requirements of (her) degree program and (my) professorship.

> Yes. My first (now ended) relationship with the father of my first born suffered for many reasons but one was the fact I was working on getting tenure during that time. Being an academic mom also comes with challenges that I don't see my male colleagues (who are also parents) face. They have a wife/mom at home therefore they are more able to network after normal work hours and travel more frequently. I've turned down research opportunities because I'm a parent, plus any long-term residency opportunities are a "no way"!

Question: Has the decision to parent while in academia impacted your overall happiness?

Responses:

> Yes, I used to love my career. Since having my son, I often feel punished, judged, and overlooked because I am now a parent. Logistically, it has also felt impossible to pick up where I left off, especially because my son was born during the pandemic.

> Both of my children have been profoundly and positively affected by being "Professor's Kids", which has helped them grow into broadly curious, inquisitive, skeptical and responsible young people.

> Parenting fills me with meaning and purpose. Gives me needed balance from work and forces me to shut off the computer and spend time with my family. I feel like it makes me more understanding of my students and other people who have family needs.

> I've started to see a therapist.

> Parenting makes me happier overall. Parenting makes me less happy with academia.

Question: Anything else you'd like to add?

Responses:

> I don't subscribe to the theory that academics must be so fully committed to their jobs that they don't have time for a family or a life. I reject the notion that having a family makes you less committed as an academic—I think the opposite is true. However, I still fall prey to these myths in the way that I regard myself as an academic and the way I show up as a teacher and colleague. The dominant culture in my department tells me I'm not doing what I'm supposed to be doing. The system is not set up to reward me for going against it.

> If you're going to be an effective parent-cum-academician, you need to enable yourself to live an incredibly adaptive daily life.

> If you're reading this and you're worried about promotion and you have a kid under 5, and you're the primary parent, I feel for you. Even before the pandemic, it was impossible.

> My spouse is military, and nothing outweighs that in our home. He deploys; we have no say. The university can tell me I don't do enough research, but they won't tell me I'm an excellent mom and sometimes dad.

> Pre-COVID the scales were unbalanced regarding parenting in academia. Now parenting in academia during a pandemic, I feel I'm off the scale altogether. I'm not unhappy, but that is only because I've become conditioned to accept it...I am grateful to be working and to be with my child. My career, however, feels like it's one foot in the grave.

29

FINAL THOUGHTS

Institutions of higher learning must supply the scaffolding to support families with and without children in order to retain and support their faculty. How do institutions stand to benefit from these changes? For starters, these systems help recruit and retain talent by creating environments where research and practice can flourish, and where faculty can grow. Additionally, the parent/caregiver perspective can be uniquely flexible and empathetic to support learners in ways that have direct impact on student success and retention, particularly among first generation college students. More direct support for parents and caregivers within academia would increasingly power diversity within higher education and be more reflective of the range of perspectives and diversity within industry and the workforce.[11] Research indicates that the majority of faculty in the US have children and/or get married. Most of the efforts to support academic families have historically been made at four-year universities, however not all faculty who would benefit from this support work at four-year universities.

In addition to acknowledgement of faculty needs and mentorship backed by institutional support, there are clear structural redesigns to help level the playing field: paid family leave, a flexible workplace, a flexible career track, a re-entry policy, pay equity reviews, childcare assistance, and dual-career assistance. Companies that have put such policies in place have seen benefits of recruitment and retention, and some universities have taken notice. For instance, after UC Berkeley enacted several policies in 2013 to benefit parents including paid teaching leave for fathers, job satisfaction among parents scored much higher and more babies were born to assistant professors[12].

But the kinds of policies at UC Berkley are a long way from reality for many in academia, and several survey respondents indicated a grave outlook on their research and careers during the COVID-19 pandemic. So, how do we support our parent colleagues today? As we continue to inquire into the culture and expectations in academia as it relates to parenting, the presence of community and allyship are vital. Allyship from colleagues and coworkers to be part of the conversation about work-life balance, or how a department considers the responsibilities of colleagues who have children or caregiver roles. Community in organizations like Artist/Parent/Academic[13] or the Parent Artist Advocacy League[14], both of which support parents in the arts and academia presenting a variety of family-friendly residencies, national crit groups, research opportunities, childcare grants, external funding, and more.

This conversation is on-going and this paper attempts to add to the topic by sharing perspectives from those who have experience parenting, caregiving, and working in academia during and prior to the COVID-19 pandemic. Please contact the author if you'd like to collaborate in this research. Now is the time to examine the range of institutional benefits in normalizing parenting and caregiving alongside academic work before the impact of social distancing is forgotten.

CITATIONS

Clapp, E. (Director). (n.d.). *The Perilous Texas Adventures of Mark Dion* [Video file]. Retrieved from https://www.amazon.com/Perilous-Texas-Adventures-Mark-Dion/dp/B0891S3HTD

Bassett, R. H. (2005). *Parenting and professing: Balancing family work with an academic career.* Nashville: Vanderbilt University Press.

June Member Survey: The burden is real - immediate action needed to support and retain working parents. (2021, January 19) Retrieved from https://hicleo.com/blog/the-burden-is-real-immediate-action-needed-to-support-and-retain-working-parents/

Vesoulis, A. (2020, September 08). How COVID-19 is Decimating the Daycare Industry. Retrieved from https://time.com/5886491/covid-childcare-daycare/

Quilantan, B. (2020, September 14). How the pandemic is upending pre-K. Retrieved from https://www.politico.com/newsletters/weekly-education-coronavirus-special-edition/2020/09/14/how-the-pandemic-is-upending-pre-k-790370

Erprose. (2020, December 22). Second stimulus checks will help, but U.S. income crisis runs much deeper than Covid. Retrieved from https://www.cnbc.com/2020/12/20/second-stimulus-checks-help-but-income-crisis-bigger-than-covid-.html

Bozkurt, Tülay & Ozden, Melis. (2010). The relationship between empathetic classroom climate and students' success. Procedia - Social and Behavioral Sciences. 5. 231–234. 10.1016/j.sbspro.2010.07.078.

Flaherty, C. (2020, August 11). Babar in the Room. Retrieved from https://www.insidehighered.com/news/2020/08/11/faculty-parents-are-once-again-being-asked-perform-miracle

Tigg, F. (2019, September 26). Professor Carries Student's Baby for 3-Hour Lecture So Mother Can Concentrate and Take Notes. Retrieved from https://www.complex.com/life/2019/09/professor-carries-student-baby-3-hour-lecture

Schroeder, R. (2020, December 11). Mental Health Epidemic: Dark Shadow of the COVID Pandemic. Retrieved from https://www.insidehighered.com/digital-learning/blogs/online-trending-now/mental-health-epidemic-dark-shadow-covid-pandemic

SCHOU, S. (2020, April 14). Raising Consciousness: Diversity in Graphic Design. Retrieved from http://www.artcenter.edu/connect/dot-magazine/articles/diversity-graphic-design.html

Mason, M. (2015, August 5). The Baby Penalty. Retrieved from https://www.chronicle.com/article/the-baby-penalty/

30

Artist/Parent/Academic. (n.d.). Retrieved from https://laurenfrancesevans.com/artistparentacademic

Parent Artist Advocacy League (PAAL) for Performing Arts and Media. (n.d.). Retrieved from https://www.paalthe-atre.com/

APPENDIX A.
List of Survey Questions Asked

THE BEGINNING

1) **How long have you been teaching in academia?**

    a) Under 1 year

    b) 1-3 years

    c) 3-6 years

    d) 6+ years

2) **Please select all that apply to your position:**

    a) full time

    b) tenured

    c) tenure-track

    d) adjunct

    e) instructor

    f) professor of practice

    g) endowed instructor

    h) visiting instructor

    i) write-in

3) **Please select the type of institution(s) that most aligns with where you teach. Select as many as you need.**

    a) Research-focused 4-year college or university

    b) Teaching-focused 4-year college or university

    c) Historically Black College or University

    d) Community College

    e) Write-in

4) **Are you partnered with or married to someone who teaches full time in academia?**

    a) Yes

    b) No

    c) It's Complicated

5) **If you are partnered with or married to someone who teaches full time in academia, please select the type of institution(s)** that most aligns with where they teach. Select as many as you need.

    a) We both work at the same institution.

    b) Research-focused 4-year college or university

    c) Teaching-focused 4-year college or university

    d) Historically Black College or University

    e) Community College

    F) N/A

    g) write-in

6) **If you are partnered with or married to someone who teaches full time in academia, please select all that apply to their position.**

    a) full time

    b) tenured

    c) tenure-track

    d) adjunct

    e) instructor

    f) professor of practice

    g) endowed instructor

    h) visiting instructor

    i) N/A

    j) write-in

THE MIDDLE

7) On a scale of 0 to 10, what impact has the response to virtual, hybrid, or hyflex instruction due to COVID-19 had on your teaching? 0 = teaching duties decreased, 10 = teaching duties increased.

8) On a scale of 0 to 10, what impact has the response to virtual, hybrid, or hyflex instruction due to COVID-19 had on your research? 0 = research duties decreased, 10 = research duties increased.

9) On a scale of 0 to 10, what impact has the response to virtual, hybrid, or hyflex instruction due to COVID-19 had on your service? 0 = service duties decreased, 10 = service duties increased.

10) **Please indicate the level of change in your duties as a caregiver and/or parent.**

    a) no change at all

    b) some change, but not greatly impacting my ability to work

    c) some change, which has greatly impacted my ability to work

    d) a lot of change, which has greatly impacted my ability to work

11) **Are you a primary caregiver and/or parent?**

    a) yes

    b) no

    c) care is split evenly between myself and at least one other person

    d) write-in

12) **With 1 as the lowest rating, please rate your work environment based on their support for caregivers and/or parents prior to COVID-19.** 1= not supportive prior to COVID-19, 5 = very supportive prior to COVID-19

13) **With 1 as the lowest rating, please rate your work environment based on their support for caregivers and/or parents since COVID-19.** 1= not supportive since to COVID-19, 5 = very supportive since to COVID-19

THE END

14) Has the decision to parent while in academia influenced your partnership and career? If so, how?

15) Has the decision to parent while in academia impacted your overall happiness? How so?

16) Anything else you'd like to add?

SHORT PAPER

Racially Insensitive Visualizations: The Shortcomings of Presenting Data as Human Forms

EUGENE PARK

Associate Professor,
University of Minnesota,
Twin Cities, Minnesota, USA

Keywords
data visualization, information
design, icon-based visualizations,
decolonization, inclusive design,
design history

Effective visualizations on population data can help reveal insights into societal and systematic problems and even offer possible solutions. Despite all of the utilitarian benefits that conventional forms of visualizations can provide, designers and mathematicians alike have offered new modes of representing data by shaping graphs into the likeness of humans. One of the impetuses behind these modes of representations is rooted in the idea that when reduced to numbers, bars, lines, and dots, humans are stripped of their identities and individualities in favor of an empirical view of the world. This view is shared by Jacob Harris (2015) who explained how conventional graphs representing demographics can remove viewers from empathizing with the human subjects that are being quantified, and he proposed visualizing such data into the likeness of humans as a possible solution. While the motivations and approaches to these experimental and anthropomorphic forms of data-driven graphics raise important questions and novel opportunities, some of the resulting visualizations have unfortunately yielded problematic portrayals of BIPOC groups. What these shortcomings show is the implicit bias and the shortsightedness in the field of data visualization that can serve as important lessons to its practitioners. They can teach us that any attempt to construct new forms of visualizations—particularly those that resemble human figures—must be sensitive and inclusive to all peoples. In this opinion article, the shortcomings of two data-driven graphics, ISOTYPE and Chernoff Faces, will be examined. The intention behind this critique is not to suggest that the efforts of anthropomorphized visualizations is a self-defeating ambition, but to help promote inclusive design practices for practitioners of the field.

First proposed in the 1920s, Otto Neurath and Gerd Arntz's pictograph system, International System of Typographic Picture Education (ISOTYPE), had a lasting impact in the history of art and design. Decades after its creation, ISOTYPE's influence continued to resonate in the work of modern-day data/information visualizations, one of which was even published by the New York Times to visualize the casualties of the Iraq War in 2007 (Albuquerque & Cheng, 2008). On a formal level, the ambition of ISOTYPE, and the craftsmanship that follows it are historically significant. When examined closer, however, it becomes apparent that there are racial prejudices embedded into the design of Neurath and Arntz's pictograph system that reduce people of color into their racial and cultural stereotypes. In Neurath's 1936 publication containing some of the first specimens of ISOTYPE, culturally oversimplified depictions of BIPOC people that include Mexican and Hispanic men with sombreros and Asians with conical hats are present (p. 47). In addition to the stereotypes that are in full display in the pictograms, there is also an oversimplification in the enumeration of different groups of non-white people around the world. Ruben Pater (2016) observes that the number of non-white races represented in ISOTYPE is a mere 4 groups, which undermines the objectivity that Neurath claimed his pictogram system to have

32

(p. 131). This effort to establish conglomerates of races, not just in label, but also in appearance demonstrates the moral disregard and racial prejudice behind the historically celebrated pictograph system. The conflating of races into a few broad groups reduces the diversity of humans into simplified categories and also mythologizes people of color. Naomi Mezey (2013) of Georgetown Law Center writes that the census is the power to categorize and count populations because it grants the privilege to recognize, exclude, and even erase certain groups (p. 1713). Similar to conducting a census, the infographics in ISOTYPE that depicts global populations is an exercise of power that colonizes those that do not fit into the mold of white Europeans into categories of otherness that obfuscates identities and diversities. Populations carry multitudes and any attempts to visualize its contents must work towards revealing the dignities of all people, and the shortcomings of ISOTYPE stand as a reminder of the complexities and delicacies of quantifying people through graphical means. This is not to suggest that ISOTYPE be expelled from design history curriculums but to urge instructors in these courses to bring the topic into new light and impress upon students on the consequences that designs, just like words, have consequences.

A Chernoff Face, also known as face symbols, is a visualized dataset in the form of a human face. First proposed in 1973 by Herman Chernoff, a statistician from Stanford University, up to 18 different facial features, such as angle of eyebrow, radius of the ear, and length of the nose, can be used to represent multivariable datasets. Several examples of Chernoff Faces are presented in Figure 1. The proposed advantage of utilizing Chernoff Faces is to provide a familiar visual to compare and contrast different groups of categorical datasets. There are no correct methodologies or standards set in place

for creating the specifications of new Chernoff Faces, and practitioners are free to set their own parameters and decide which facial features are connected to the dataset and how they are presented.

Unlike ISOTYPE, whose pictographs are composed of elements meant to represent different groups of people, Chernoff Faces do not depict specific racial and ethnic groups. Under the wrong conditions, however, these visuals can still cause harm towards people of color. For instance, the variables for adjusting the eye sizes and angles, under extreme values, can yield offensive displays of Asian caricatures with exaggerated narrow eyes that evoke the racist portrayals of Asians, specifically Japanese Americans during World War II. The possibility that Chernoff Faces can produce similar offensive depictions was unfortunately realized in 2008 when the New York Times published a set of Chernoff Faces that visualized the performances of Major League Baseball (MLB) managers from the 2007 season (Wang, 2008). Some of the resulting faces, specifically the ones designated to visualize the performances of Bob Green, Bob Melvin, and Ron Washington have resulted in the aforementioned offensive depictions. The visualization was somehow removed from the Times' article page but can still be seen in their online archives (ibid). Whether this was intentional or not, it is unfortunate that a novel visualization tool that seeks to provide new ways to present data can also possess visual traits that perpetuate racist stereotypes, leading to unintended effects. Since practitioners have the freedom to choose how their datasets are ultimately presented, Chernoff Faces have a history of yielding results that are sometimes comically exaggerated to the point of illegibility. The original guidelines set by Herman Chernoff can result in faces where certain features can

variable 1: eyebrow angle
variable 2: eye width
variable 3: eye angle
variable 4: nose width
variable 5: mouth width
variable 6: mouth curvature
variable 7: head width

Figure 1: *Examples of Chernoff Faces using a randomized dataset. Seven variables are visualized through different facial features. Graphic created by the author in 2020.*

become enlarged to the point where other parts of the face become difficult to view (Nelson, 2007, p. 57). Mathematical adjustments and normalization methods can help alleviate these problems but anticipating potentially unclear outcomes and even offensive displays of people requires expertise that goes beyond the proficiency of representing data with graphical clarity.

For novel and unconventional visualizations to be effective, particularly those that resemble human features, thorough testing should be implemented before proposing them for widespread use. Under these tests, one should not be singularly focused on measuring accessibility and efficiency of the graphics but should also make sure that all of its variations and permutations do not offend or exclude any group. Conducting focus groups with diverse representations can also help with detecting potential stereotypes and offensive displays. Chernoff faces can benefit from testing out the lower and upper bounds of their categories to detect potential flaws in the displays of their facial features.

Beyond these tests, what is also needed is a set of values that codifies the ethics behind the presentation of data. Alberto Cairo (2014) addresses this topic from a journalism perspective and offers the argument that designers should refrain from creating visualizations that are unable to transmit information efficiently, because the decision to willfully choose a graph that provides less clarity is an immoral choice that leaves viewers confused and uninformed (p. 27). Utilizing data-driven graphics that are offensive to people of color is also an immoral choice, because not only do they distract audiences from understanding the data, but they also perpetuate the racial/ethnic misconceptions that are not supported by any body of evidence. Design is an enterprise that strives to enhance the thriving of human life, not denigrate it with falsehoods and poorly tested products/systems. As practitioners and educators participating in this field, we must do better in our respective practices to ensure that the data that we display are accessible to the target audience(s) and inoffensive towards everyone.

William S. Cleveland (1987), an early pioneer in data visualization, wrote that "[i]nventing a graphical method is easy. Inventing one that works is difficult" (p. 420). There is indeed a challenge in creating novel forms of data visualization that are clear and useful, but we need to go beyond the functional requirements of the field and seek to offer new forms of knowledge that aren't solely focused on emulating humanity but respecting it. Data visualization is a specialty that demands much technical knowledge in statistics, but integrating it with inclusive design practices and a decolonizing mindset can help usher the field away from the perpetual cycles of historical ignorance and implicit bias.

REFERENCES:

Albuquerque, A. L. de, & Cheng, A. (2008, January 6). Opinion | A Year in Iraq (Published 2008). *The New York Times*. https://www.nytimes.com/2008/01/06/opinion/06chart.html

Cairo, A. (2014). Ethical Infographics: In Data Visualziation, Journalism Meets Engineering. *IRE Journal*, 37(2), 25–27. Academic Search Premier.

Cleveland, W. S. (1987). Research in Statistical Graphics. Journal of the *American Statistical Association*, 82(398), 419–423. JSTOR. https://doi.org/10.2307/2289443

Harris, J. (2015, January 15). *Connecting with the Dots—Learning - Source: An OpenNews project*. Connecting with the Dots: Jake Harris on Data Visualization, Empathy, and Representing People with Dots. https://source.opennews.org/articles/connecting-dots/

Mezey, N. (2003). Erasure and Recognition: The Census, Race and the National Imagination. *Northwestern University Law Review*, 97(4), 1701–1768. Academic Search Premier.

Nelson, E. S. (2007). The Face Symbol: Research Issues and Cartographic Potential. *Cartographica*, 42(1), 53–64. Academic Search Alumni Edition.

Neurath, O. (1936). *International picture language: The first rules of Isotype*. London : K. Paul, Trench, Trubner & co., ltd.

Pater, R. (2016). *The politics of design: A (not so) global manual for visual communication*. BIS Publishers.

Wang, S. C. (2008). Smile if You Bunt. *The New York Times*. https://archive.nytimes.com/www.nytimes.com/imagepages/2008/04/01/science/20080401_PROF_GRAPHIC.html?action=click&module=RelatedCoverage&pgtype=Article&region=Footer

34

SHORT PAPER

Revisionist History

KRISTEN COOGAN

Associate Professor Graphic Design,
Chair Graduate Graphic Design,
Boston University,
Boston, Massachusetts, USA

Keywords
pedagogy, history, democratic,
revisionist, egalitarian

A pandemic. Racial reckoning. Civil unrest. Political uprising. For many of us, the year 2020 motivated self-examination across every spectrum of our consciousness — social, cultural, economic and intellectual.

Academia provided space for impact. We had to pivot suddenly, adapting an in person pedagogy to one that would operate remotely — we were building the plane while flying. My impulse to instruct remotely was at first off-base. The students clearly needed time to adjust to the improbability of it all. And so we traded leads; we flattened the pedagogical hierarchy. An egalitarian architecture materialized where students led and I followed.

Students felt fragile, we all did, as individuals seeking to normalize mammoth instability. This vulnerability underscored the value of inclusivity, all voices deserved a platform. Was my pedagogy inclusive enough? Was it empathic enough? How did it speak to our social and political context that was under intense scrutiny? Instead of a pedagogy informed by my own lived experiences, a bias especially visible in my Graphic Design History curriculum, I wondered what would inspire students to independently ask the same important questions we are reflecting on in this publication.

Academia faces an opportunity and graphic design history, in particular, is under fire. But how was its white-washed history bathed in exclusivity established in the first place? One hundred years ago, graphic design history emerged as an off-shoot to the practice and was codified by the industry with European trade books such as Jan Tschichold's *Die Neue Typographie*, Alfred Tolmer's *Mise en Page*, and periodicals including *Neue Grafik, Arts et Metier Graphique, Gebrauchsgraphik, Typographiche Mitteilungen* and more. The economics fueling the discipline relegated graphic design to either commercial audiences defined by and for privileged classes or as a beacon for mobilization, whether political, existential or otherwise. 'During the 1950s graphic design history gradually emerged as pedagogy and art museum curators began to collect graphic design ephemera and acquired papers and artifacts. Graphic design history books became accessible to wider audiences through a rise in classes, symposia and conferences.' (Heller, 2020) The 1980s saw a groundswell of historical and theoretical inquiry driven by the emergence and proliferation of MFA Graphic Design programs in the United States and a tradition of graphic design scholarship firmly situated itself within the academy. American Philip Meggs released *A History of Graphic Design* in 1983, documenting the presence of visual communication dating back to ancient Egypt. Trade magazines including London's *Eye* and California's *Emigre* were decisive counterpoints to Meggs's preeminent narrative. Fast forward to the digital revolution when tools for creating, consuming and distributing content were ubiquitous, the discourse took a hard right. In 2001 Wikipedia, followed by Facebook, Instagram, Twitter, and self-publishing ventures completely democratized authorship and accessibility. When social media and self-publishing ventures enabled greater access to tools for content consumption and production, visual culture itself ballooned,

35

Figure 1: Peruvian Chicha street graphics snub elite aesthetic credo, acting as vehicles for anti-establishment, anti-colonial expression. "Wall Drawings, icônes urbaines". 2016. (MAC Lyon Francia Gallery). Illustration from https://www.elliottupac.com/sarigrafias_1/ [accessed June 21, 2021])

removing any notion of absolutism. Which brings us to today, a discourse ripe for interrogation, reinvention and expansion.

But, how does this culture of critique shape a historical survey? Developing a Graphic Design History curriculum affirms a perspective with every Google slide. My initial set of images and accompanying narrative represented just one vision — mine. The story I've chronicled hinges on the presence of design cycles throughout the past two centuries. Within each subject, I endeavor to pinpoint a narrow design consciousness that galvanized broader, cross-disciplinary outcomes. For instance, during the industrial revolution, design was articulated as a discrete thought process, creating a deeper division between the user and the maker. Seventy-five years later Buckminster Fuller's dymaxion car regarded objectivity and purpose over all else and ushered in a culture of streamlining. While the discourse meanders from architecture, to industrial design, to branding, to typography, the lectures follow a template identifying the initial design seed that germinates into design objects and experiences. We trace the presence of design concepts that mutate from the academy or a place of experimentation, to the commercial and consumer mainstream. While my narrative reflects a chronology of key visual and conceptual histories, the story is never complete and, I believe, should be rewritten

collectively; participation, integration and expansion yields the requisite inclusivity. Design history is fluid and mutable; it could, and should, be in a constant state of revision. Reimagining this history requires regular dialogue, attention, dissent, and revision by the population it serves — educators, students, and practitioners.

Recognizing the universal need to decolonize the design history narrative recently triggered multiple efforts resulting in varying forms of expansion. Our student audiences are growing increasingly more diverse and represent cultures that deserve acknowledgement. Projects such as *The People's Graphic Design Archive* (Sandhaus & Levit, 2020), Polymode's *Bipoc Design History* (Polymode, 2021) and Bahia Shehab's and Haytham Nawar's *A History of Arab Graphic Design* (Shehab & Nawar, 2020) provide important additions. Questioning assumptions is vital to our work as educators, artists and designers and decolonizing graphic design history requires more than challenging the Eurocentric narratives of art and design. We need a model to continue advancing design history — a democratic versus absolutist style of inquiry where individual perspectives comprise our design history fabric. In this proposed model, the design history narrative adapts to its audience, and fosters inclusivity, through a redistributed dialogue. Levelling the pedagogical hierarchy democratizes the conversation, stimulating deep

36

understanding, helping to uncover our student's individualized points of view. The importance of showing, discussing, and including artists, designers, and writers who represent people, cultures, and aesthetics historically excluded from history textbooks reveals visual culture minorities who created influential, context specific work. The egalitarian nature of these missing conversations translates to the content itself: everything matters.

Adopting this model as a form of design history pedagogy runs the risk of compromising qualitative standards. Although 'good design' is a subjective and culturally specific concept, educators should be mindful of helping students develop a process for supplementing the design canon. When educators illuminate context, and indicate the cycle of design from conceptual origin, to pragmatic artifact, to cultural reception, and then finally commercial mainstream, students gain a historic awareness that they can apply to their own curation. Mapping this process throughout design history establishes a thought pattern that equips students with the criticality needed to identify 'good design'. Stimulating these new student perspectives shaped by individualized cultural backgrounds and lived experiences begins with analysis and curation — students simultaneously learned mine and developed their own unique points of view. Our weekly discussions comprised groups of eight to ten students led by a subset of two or three students. These facilitators fostered conversations to identify blind spots or cultural equivalents absent from that week's lectures and readings. At a fundamental level, students were encouraged to consider, interrogate and generate alternative content derived from their own set of preferences, experiences and inclinations. After just one semester, these gaps yielded rich new additions, disrupted the canonical hierarchy and exposed 'low vernacular' visual styles that are realizing renewed seriousness.

My students and I tested this model during Fall 2020. With the conceptual, and contextual, process outlined above in mind, students linked Victorian era broadsides to contemporary Peruvian culture. We began by reflecting on industrialization and the separation of design as an isolated planning activity, a condition that spawned a multitude of aftershocks

within our 19th century visual landscape. Victorian eclecticism permeated furniture design, consumer products, fashion and even typography. Style emerged as a symbolic idea, denoting class and worth with every extraneous flourish. Form signified status. The Victorian broadside offered another application for extravagant ornamentation, expressed through motley compositions of Egyptian, serif and sans serif typography. Posters looked this way because they were trying to grab the attention of someone wading through the city among all the other printed posters and advertisements. The design with the most ostentatious typography often "won". Fast forward one hundred years, and the competition for a user's attention persisted throughout the streets of Los Angeles (until 2012) with the Colby Poster tradition. Adding fluorescent ink colors to the familiar typographic bric-a-brac seen in 19th street art, Colby Posters displayed a "lowbrow approach result[ing] in a minimal, bold, and no-nonsense aesthetic that was always eye-catching and surprising" (Dunne, 2014). A Lima, Peru based student learning remotely during Fall 2020 was able to connect this work with posters she sees in her own daily environment. Peruvian Chicha street graphics snub elite aesthetic credo, acting as vehicles for anti-establishment, anti-colonial expression (Figure 1). The anti-purist posters incorporate Andean-influenced fluorescent colors, performative typography and idiosyncratic iconography, evoking a positive expression of diversity, medley and democracy (Neira, 2016). The more is more mentality transcends generations, classes and technology, and is indiscriminate towards its audience, amplifying its inclusive appeal. These relics of lowly street culture dovetail their noble origins, blurring the lines between elite and vernacular design. Lorraine Wild's Great Wheel of Style progresses at whiplash speed. Low is high; high is low (Sandhaus, 2000).

Another important side story came to light during the Fall 2020 experiment, when my many students from China highlighted another compelling example absent from the Western canon. Communist propaganda is regularly featured in the telling of design history. We know that Russian Constructivism branded the Communist regime. Like the Peruvian Chicha artists, the Soviet Union similarly

37

Figure 2: Scatter the old world, build the new, from late 1960s (IISH/ Stefan R Landsberger Collections). Illustration from https://www. bbc.com/news/world-asia-china-24923993 (accessed June 21, 2021)

addressed a universal audience, codifying a Communist aesthetic expressed with bold red and black geometric abstractions designed to cross classes, dialects and geographies. Every black square, red wedge and instance of pictorial typography stimulated institutional loyalty: messages were meant to be seen, heard and revered. "Dynamically composed forms conjure a vision of the new world, 'constructed' through a new visual architecture" (Coogan, 2020). My students in the class from China drew a parallel between the Communist propaganda and the lesser known, Big Character Posters (Dazibao), which carried a similar aesthetic and political gravity. Like Communist Propaganda, the posters fervently entrenched a new political ideal, fortifying China's 1960s Cultural Revolution led by Mao Zedong. Featuring bold black and red palettes and agitated typography hearkening to Constructivist visual language, the Big Character Posters "established a forum for discussion and dissemination" but were ultimately weaponized against their own grass-roots audience (Figure 2) (Ho, 2017). "Big-character posters were … ubiquitous, used for everything from sophisticated debate to satirical entertainment

to rabid denunciation; being attacked in a big-character poster was enough to end one's career" (Dazibao, n.d.). The generations surviving the Cultural Revolution reacted to political pressure and suppressed their own appalling first-hand experiences, inadvertently obscuring the Dazibao culture in its entirety. A 2017 Harvard University exhibition featuring Dazibao posters presented over fifty works donated anonymously. Chinese historians involved in the curation noted their own abbreviated awareness stemming from a lack of information — a culture of secrecy prolonged by relatives and educators who were likely pawns pressured by the regime to incriminate or abuse their own community (Bergeron, 2017). Expanding our design history discourse simultaneously unearths, activates and repairs, allowing us to collectively process a past etched in trauma.

 It's critical that we adopt a more inclusive, egalitarian method for studying and shaping graphic design history as we acknowledge the populations who have been or still are marginalized by current modules. The examples outlined here legitimize that approach, as they uniformly oppose absolutist traditions that routinely glorified idols and instead reflect the diverse, non-Western audiences sitting in our classrooms. Student generated content opens new possibilities "that are increasingly inclusive, representative and varied" (Rittner, 2020). Charged with identifying cultural equivalents that shared conceptual and contextual themes, students supplemented the canon with lesser known examples that broaden design history. Democratizing methods for establishing design history narratives validates visual cultures that were historically excluded and provides space for our audience to incorporate their own important cultural legacies—like the Peruvian Chicha and Chinese Big Character Posters. As design educators and students, we owe a debt to visual culture, to reflect on and contextualize more homespun visual chapters. Our student audiences are only growing more global and diverse — let's reorient the historical landscape and embrace a messier, more inclusive terrain. Liberate idiosyncrasies and embrace authenticity. We run the risk of over-complicating design history, but we endow our future discourse with an inclusivity that our students and our discipline deserves.

BIBLIOGRAPHY

Bergeron, Chris. "Harvard exhibit showcases Chinese posters hidden for 50 years." *Wicked Local*, New Media Investment Group, 19 November 2017, https://cambridge.wickedlocal.com/entertainmentlife/20171119/harvard-exhibit-showcases-chinese-posters-hidden-for-50-years. Accessed 12 January 2021.

Coogan, Kristen. "Knowing Your Design History is Crucial to Aesthetic Innovation." *AIGA Eye on Design*, AIGA, 22 June 2020, https://eyeondesign.aiga.org/knowing-your-design-history-is-crucial-to-aesthetic-innovation/. Accessed 5 January 2021.

"Dazibao." *Wikipedia*, Wikipedia, https://en.wikipedia.org/wiki/Big-character_poster. Accessed 11 January 2021.

Dunne, Carey. "In Memory Of Colby, The L.A. Print Shop That Made Posters For Jimi Hendrix, The Sex Pistols, And Ed Ruscha." *Fast Company*, Mansueto Ventures, 15 January 2014, https://www.fastcompany.com/3024514/the-guerilla-graphics-of-colby-poster-printing-company. Accessed 6 January 2021.

Heller, Steven. "Crowd Sourcing Graphic Design History." Design Observer, *Design Observer*, 29 July 2020, https://designobserver.com/feature/crowd-sourcing-graphic-design-history/40295. Accessed 15 January 2021.

Ho, Denise. "Exhibiting the Cultural Revolution, Part 1: Reading "Big-Character Posters."" *Medium*, A Medium Corporation, 7 November 2017, https://medium.com/fairbank-center/exhibiting-the-cultural-revolution-part-1-reading-big-character-posters-d3edd7bb0104. Accessed 11 January 2021.

Neira, E. "Peruvian Chicha Phenomenon And The Subversion Of Taste." *Arts in a Changing America*, ArtChangeUS, 1 June 2016, https://artsinachangingamerica.org/peruvian-chicha-phenomenon-subversiondecolonization-taste/. Accessed 3 December 2020.

Polymode. "*BIPOC DESIGN HISTORY.*" BIPOC DESIGN HISTORY, Polymode, 1 January 2021, https://bipocdesignhistory.com/. Accessed 15 January 2021.

Rittner, Jennifer. "Teaching Design History." *dcrit*, School of Visual Arts, 28 January 2020, https://dcrit.medium.com/teaching-design-history-e0ad6c5fd72c. Accessed 21 January 2021.

Sandhaus, Louise. "Reputations: Lorraine Wild." *Eye Magazine*, Eye Magazine Ltd., Summer 2000, http://www.eyemagazine.com/feature/article/reputations-lorraine-wild. Accessed 14 January 2020.

Sandhaus, Louise, and Briar Levit. "*The People's Graphic Design Archive.*" The People's Graphic Design Archive, The People's Graphic Design Archive, 1 July 2020, https://www.peoplesgdarchive.org/. Accessed 15 January 2021.

Shehab, Bahia, and Haytham Nawar. A *History of Arab Graphic Design*. Cairo, The American University in Cairo Press, 2020. *Arab Lit*, https://arablit.org/2020/11/19/bahia-shehab-on-a-history-of-arab-graphic-design/. Accessed 17 January 2021.

SHORT PAPER

Diverse and Inclusive Strategies for Crisis Management in the Design classroom

LINH DAO

Assistant Professor,
California Polytechnic State University,
San Luis Obispo, California, USA

Keywords
crisis management, diversity,
inclusion, agile design, curriculum
design, pandemic

ABSTRACT

In this paper, I will be discussing the development of management, mobility, and adaptation skills as an important part of the professional practice being taught in the classroom, especially in times of crisis such as Covid-19. This paper introduces strategies to effectively mitigate the effects of Covid-19. They include rethinking the format of the class, preferred teaching approaches, the method of delivery, and the content of the curriculum, taking into consideration the needs of students with less privileged and disadvantaged backgrounds.

Many working creative professionals can recall the dot-com bust or the recent recession. The intersection of public health and the economic crisis that came with the recent pandemic, however, is an unprecedented scenario in many ways (Andersen 2020). The wide ramifications of student existing struggles, especially those who belong to disadvantaged communities, commanded special attention to the skills that students need to acquire in addition to design. This paper introduces practical strategies to develop those skills and mitigate the effects of the pandemic in the classroom.

The pandemic has exposed many of the hidden struggles that my students have. Resulted disparities and limited access to health services have led to rising rate of depression and anxiety (Coe 2020), economic hardships (Allen 2021), lack of internet access at home or an adequate study place (Aristovnik 2020), and compounded racial disparities in learning and achievement (Dorn 2020). The sizable gaps in impact by race, class and institution type, allowed white and middle-class students to take the same amount of classes while their peers of less privileged background struggled to maintain their plans of study and graduate on time (Inside Higher Ed, 2020). They found themselves working on even less – less time, less energy, less attention, and less support. These challenges made clear that the standard policy of giving deadline extensions to students is insufficient. They called for a more holistic approach to provide students with the resources and support that they need, including the development of important skills such as management, mobility, and adaptation.

The following development strategies were created in my classroom with the help of student responses through participation in polls and surveys. These strategies were first introduced as a result of Covid-19 to adapt to the unique format and content of my classroom for virtual delivery. They were later formalized and refined to become a permanent part of my curriculum for how versatile they are.

MANAGEMENT SKILL

Management skill helps students preemptively cope with unexpectedness and emergencies, some of which are more devastating for first generation and disadvantaged students. Extensive surveying in my classes pointed out that most of my students encountered issues with inadequate self-esteem, family

40

support, and motivation. These issues have taken the form of late assignment submissions, inconsistent or nonexistent communication, low engagement, and difficulties locating and utilizing course materials. Some of these patterns are aligned with the national trends of barriers for first-generation students (Heath 2020), which make up a large number of students in my class.

Therefore, developing management skills has become a permanent part of the content of my interaction design I & II classes. They are included in the demonstration on general professional practice in the forms of:

> Project management, adjustment, and manifestation in the form of planning, scheduling, and reminders.

> Effective time tracking using no-cost and easy techniques such as notetaking.

> Task prioritization during a crisis requires students to set realistic expectations, communicate their progress, and negotiate their perfectionism.

> The craft of file storage, organization, and distribution including advanced techniques on multiple location backups, syncing, naming, and sharing files.

Crisis management and design in crisis are also included in the assignment briefs. The submission and completion of the components below are counted toward the grade:

> An agile and evolving design document as a replacement for the traditional process book. While the traditional process book is usually turned in with the project submission, the agile design document is turned in at the start of the project. It is continuously modified as the project evolves.

> A shared and continuously updated design system as a depository for group work. In the case of a group mate missing, the rest of the group will have access to their prior work.

MOBILITY SKILL

Mobility in the time of crisis has to do with taking advantage of the virtual classroom and mitigating the effects of the lack of in-person experience in response to unexpectedness and emergencies. A large part of the mobility skills can be developed if the instructor can decentralize the classroom though rapid

adoption of new practices, new protocols, and new (collaboration) technologies (Tranel 2020) such as:

> Co-working space instead of group projects with virtual infrastructure and gentle introduction to amenities such as default community and break rooms (Kepinski 426). Instead of a web-based learning management system, we used a Slack workspace to maintain a sense of community, effective student-led individual and group discussions. Individual conversations happening on Slack are less disruptive, more direct, more organized, and come with advanced commenting features.

> Alternative delivery method for virtual classroom. Instead of Zoom meetings only, my students opted for a mix of live streaming, meetings, and private messaging. They attributed their choice to better focus on class lectures without the cameras on, more stability and faster computer performance when not using Zoom.

> Micro games such as tic-tac-toe as prompters in digital space (Kepinski 423) to give students another way to interact and build community.

> Utilizing virtual avatar and minimal response options such as emojis and reactions to engage students using a visual language that they know and appreciate.

> Enabling anonymity when possible. A report by the Office for Civil Rights found that LGBTQ students faced greater levels of anxiety and stress during the pandemic than their peers, and in general are more likely to face bullying or abuse (Office for Civil Rights, 2021).

> Individual mid-course critiques, mid-project group critiques, and daily voluntary critiques as warm-up exercises. In my experience, students were eager to give critique using these methods because of shyness and the ability to refine and edit their comments in advance. There was also a noticeable improvement in their vocabulary.

> Giving students an onboarding experience of getting to know the tools and the platform as well as its less intuitive features such as pinning or setting up reminders.

41

> Not overlooking basic accessible teaching strategies such as providing captions and/or transcripts for all videos (Hamraie, 2020).

With the right setup, students can and will develop:

> The ability to embrace different methods of communication with both the instructor and the classmates.

> The technical proficiency to utilize more powerful features of the platforms such as virtual critique.

> The capability to keep up with their peer's progress every day in class.

> The ease of participating in polls and surveys with minimal efforts during or outside of class.

> The capacity to connect to their peers in non-traditional ways outside of the classroom.

ADAPTATION SKILLS

Adaptation skills allow students to modify and adjust personal patterns of working to continue to meet the demands of the course in case of unexpectedness and emergencies. Through multiple exercises and discussions, my students practiced the ability to:

> Identify and target their personal roadblocks. There might be larger patterns of inequalities that influence some of their struggles. The instructors must be willing to make reasonable adjustments in addition in terms of expectations to ensure the core objectives of the class are still met while taking into consideration the specific circumstances that students might encounter.

> Identify their personal pattern(s) of effective working. These patterns can have specific accommodations that are necessary for them to focus and to be productive such as time(s) of the day, location, ambience, etc. Since students were working on less — less time, less energy, less attention, and less support — it is important that they use their time productively.

> Support those personal pattern(s) with a designated location and time of working. These locations might be shared with other family members or roommate(s). These time slots might be short or rare. Even so, they need to voice their needs with their families or roommates.

> Work in small chunks of time. The ability to work moderately and consistently requires students to analyze, prioritize, and if necessary, pivot. This technique allows them to become more self-reliant and in control, which are characteristics that will serve them well beyond the classroom.

> Communicate with the instructor frequently and effectively using direct and concise messages. This format keeps the students in consistent and timely communication with the instructor. The instructor can ease students into this process by starting the course with a warm-up conversation with each student, asking them about their goals, expectations, and preferences.

> Use available and open-source software and tool replacements in the case of unavailable or inadequate standard industry tools. Accessibility can be an issue either due to financial reasons or due to personal circumstances.

CONCLUSION

Design always takes place within a context, and the context of the current pandemic is an opportunity to design critically, taking into consideration that student experience is concerned with where design fits in and not the other way around. The strategies introduced above have had a significant impact on my classrooms and helped students learn important skills to cope with the pandemic and beyond.

42

REFERENCES

Allen, J. (2021, June 15). *Survey finds more than half California college students saw income decline during pandemic.* EdSource. https://edsource.org/news-updates#survey-finds-more-than-half-california-college-students-saw-income-decline-during-pandemic

Andersen, M. (2020, April 9). *I'm A Design Student—What Happens Next?* Eye on Design. https://eyeondesign.aiga.org/im-a-design-student-what-happens-next/

Aristovnik, A. (2020, August 28). *How Covid-19 pandemic affected higher education students' lives globally and in the United States | College of Business.* University of Nevada, Reno. https://www.unr.edu/business/international/blog/covid-19-affecting-students

Banaji, M. R., & Greenwald, A. G. (2016). *Blindspot: Hidden Biases of Good People* (Reprint ed.). Bantam.

Coe, E. H., & Enomoto, K. (2020, November 4). *Returning to resilience: The impact of COVID-19 on mental health and substance use.* McKinsey & Company. https://www.mckinsey.com/industries/healthcare-systems-and-services/our-insights/returning-to-resilience-the-impact-of-covid-19-on-behavioral-health

Hamraie, A. (2020, August 6). *Accessible Teaching in the Time of COVID-19.* Critical Design Lab. https://www.mapping-access.com/blog-1/2020/3/10/accessible-teaching-in-the-time-of-covid-19?fbclid=IwAR0t2ybPwND09xN-yI9AQNj1Wrhj5P9iutKhsqZpvJAMlKPI-P_UFcKhs7U

Heath, R. (2020, November 11). *Against All Odds: First-generation Students and Noncognitive Barriers.* Center for First Generation Student Success. https://firstgen.naspa.org/blog/against-all-odds-first-generation-students-and-noncognitive-barriers

Inside Higher Ed. (2020, August 4). *An analysis of data from a national survey on the impact of the pandemic.* https://www.insidehighered.com/views/2020/08/04/analysis-data-national-al-survey-impact-pandemic-higher-ed-opinion

Kepinski, L., & Nielsen, T. C. (2020). *The Inclusion Nudges Guidebook: 100 how-to behavioral designs to de-bias and make inclusive behavior, culture, and systems the default and norm.* Independently published.

Office For Civil Rights. (2021, June). *Education in a Pandemic: The Disparate Impacts of COVID-19 on America's Students.* https://www2.ed.gov/about/offices/list/ocr/docs/20210608-impacts-of-covid19.pdf

Tranel, B. (2020, July 2). *The Future Workplace Will Embrace a Hybrid Reality | Dialogue Blog | Research & Insight.* Gensler. https://www.gensler.com/blog/the-future-workplace-will-embrace-a-hybrid-reality

43

SHORT PAPER

Teaching Design in the People's Republic of China

RANDY CLARK

Assistant Professor,
Wenzhou-Kean University,
Zhejiang, Wenzhou,
Ouhai District, China

Keywords
english as a second language,
overseas education, comparing
cultures, design education

In late May of 2016, I became an Assistant Professor at an English-only university on the southern coast of China. As someone having previously taught American students in the United States for several years, I've made comparative observations between the two cultures and teaching pedagogies.

My present employer, Wenzhou-Kean University (WKU), is a Chinese government-owned institution with a cooperative agreement with Kean University in New Jersey. Although teaching in China, I am part of the faculty at Kean. We offer the same programs; teach and are governed by the same rules; issue the same grades; and share similar syllabi content, while maintaining the comparative standards of our flagship university in the United States.

Because we are Kean University/Asia, this institution also shares the same accreditations, recognitions, and degrees. Unique to our College of Architecture and Design is also our NASAD accreditation, the only institution of its kind in China.

As an American degree is highly prized in the Far East, our alumni hold a significant edge over their counterparts from native Chinese institutions of higher learning.

How does one teach graphic design in a country where most everything is so different?

Admittedly, there are challenges:

Traditions and culture. Things are done a certain way. As an example, when born into a Chinese family, grandparents pick the newborn's name. Chinese tradition is regimented and honored. There is no deviation.

All for one? Rather, one for all. While Western education focuses on the individual, in China, the emphasis is on the collective. Chinese citizens are considered an integral part of a greater cause. In other words, in the Chinese context, contribution to the collective is expected.

English-only. All instruction at this university (WKU) is taught in English. Most students at the university possess a reasonable command of English, having been taught since Kindergarten. Many are fluent. However, technical and theoretical terms are usually not understood, such as *zeitgeist, gestalt, post modernism, fibonacci,* and *nomenclature.* Many of these terms and concepts often have no translation.

Copyright, limited rights usage, and public domain.
Historically, intellectual property and copyright usage are "foreign" to the average Chinese (forgive the pun). To them, everything is considered public domain and free to use.

Typography. Chinese typography contains over 6,000 characters, each character represents a word, type is always justified, all characters are square. Kerning and leading is set on a mathematical standard of two-thirds of the square height. Everything is set in a rigid justified matrix that doesn't change.

Until recently, there was no punctuation. No hyphens, periods, commas, etc. As the average Chinese student learns English vocabulary, they become frustrated that words differ in spatial length. Capitalization is another puzzle to them. Why does a language have two sizes for the same letter? When Chinese students design with Latin-based typography, everything is set in *Helvetica Bold* (or its inferior cousin, *Arial.*). Everything is set to default: type size, kerning and leading.

Challenges, yes. But opportunities also.

Chinese students are smart. Most of our students come from wealthy families. They have been sent to the best (and most expensive) institutions, from preschool to high school. Our students have scored in the top 15% or Tier One of the Gaokao, China's version of the ACT. Being that the society places a premium on learning and memorization, most students come with a foundation of English, and the core understanding of math and science.

Chinese students are polite. They are respectful and tend to be territorial. Teachers often become second surrogate parents. Communication between former students and teacher continues past graduation.

Overall, the Chinese are very gracious. When raining, someone will insist sharing his/her umbrella. Guards on campus will follow faculty to their respective apartment to ensure safety (in a country with almost no crime). When sharing a bus ride, students will offer to pay the fare.

We had graduation not too long ago. A solid class of graphic designer graduates. After the convocation, we all met up on the stage and had pictures taken. Parents were smiling. Students were on the verge of tears, as they said their last goodbyes to their professors.

Professors are highly regarded in Chinese society. We receive discounts at movie theatres, museums, and most historic venues. The title of *Professor* is even printed on airline boarding passes.

Our university is particular as to who they hire—and retain. Once someone has established his/her value, the university does what it can to keep that faculty member happy, and keep that person here. Opera tickets, excursions to resorts (paid for by the university), dinners, shows, well-appointed

faculty lounges with massage chairs, nap rooms and sandboxes. There is even a dedicated room for faculty and staff with newborns to nurse, change diapers (which are provided) and have privacy with their children.

Chinese students are hard workers. Their culture emphasizes excellence, and students use most of their free time to study. Partying is never a problem. Few consume alcohol. On occasion, a group of students will "kidnap" their favorite teacher to eat at their favorite "hot pot" restaurant.

China has incredible museums. Every bit as impressive as the MoMA. The entire country is a living museum! Great efforts have been made to recover and preserve China's rich historical past, much of which has been rebuilt after the Cultural Revolution.

Across the road is a centuries-old Buddha monastery that has been rebuilt and restored to its former glory. Monks scurry about, as it is a place of sanctuary and a "destination" for faculty of WKU.

Chinese students possess superior rendering skills. Chinese students also are more design-conscious and perform better with an innate understanding of the grid, proportion and space.

Students come into our program already possessing strong craftsmanship and artistic skills. When student work is lavishly illustrated, one's first impression follows that the work has been plagiarized, as most American students don't have those skillsets. Chinese students do.

Chinese children enjoy the strength of the solid family unit. Men enter into retirement by age 60, and women by age 55. Those who retire receive a modest stipend similar to our Social Security. These elderly couples live with their married children in their tiny apartment.

Grandparents raise that singular grandchild while both parents work full-time. With constant supervision, children are kept on a tight leash, while pushed in the arts and other pursuits. The downside is that the child has little say in any decision-making.

Infrastructure on a local level encourages artistic development at young ages. Each "community" houses a dedicated building for

45

pursuits such as Tai Chi and dance. Present are segmented rooms for practicing the piano and other musical instruments. Often present is a small library for group study, and an exhibit celebrating the Chinese national spirit.

All communities have facilities for young students to draw, paint, and create—drawing is actively encouraged. Unlimited paper, markers, pens and pencils are available at no cost. The community bookmobile comes by weekly. All this on a national scale.

China has an online platform called "Taobao," where most people do their shopping. Taobao is a robust Ebay/Amazon equivalent online commerce site selling nearly everything.

Graffiti just isn't "a thing" in China. Neither is crime. Even in the poorest of neighborhoods, one feels safe. Companies hire artists to create murals on walls that surround construction sites. Great pains are taken to beautify spaces, malls, and parks.

So how does one motivate students to "think out of the box"?

Students respond to positive reinforcement. Much like their American counterparts, Chinese students become energized by compliments. Most students take criticism well, as long as it is couched appropriately.

Most of us who have taught in the United States can relate to a student that sabotages the learning environment. That rarely happens in China. Popular students are the ones that succeed academically. Chinese institutions do not tolerate insubordination as penalties can be harsh.

Chinese students tend to be very quiet … that is until they get to know you. Though it may bother some American teachers, a noisy class here signifies a healthy learning environment, and students who are comfortable around you.

Chinese students are not exposed to a high level of graphic design. In all fairness, neither are American students. Consequently, lots of visuals and work need be shown each class period: from Paul Rand to Stefan Sagmeister.

China is a country of contrasts. Our alphabet is phonic; theirs is pictorial. Our government is democratic; theirs is a one-party system. Our news media plays to its respective demographic audience and is essentially free of government intervention. Their news media is filtered and monitored by the government. Our homes have front and back yards with two-car garages. They have a balcony in a small high-rise apartment with their car parked in a basement garage (provided they have a car). Many of us came from large families. Most Chinese citizens are products of a government-mandated one-child family. We move away from our parents when we are older. As young Chinese people marry, their parents move in with them.

Chinese adore Americans. Taxi drivers swerve in traffic to get to you first for the honor of transporting an American. Some municipalities, such as Wenzhou, seek to recruit Americans for permanent residency. Hotels will often show foreigners special consideration.

The Chinese are fascinated with physical stature—our height, big noses, blue eyes, and blond hair. They love our movies, our music, our clothes, Kobe Bryant, and our "aura." Their culture has merged part of our culture into theirs. Have you ever heard Rap music in Mandarin?

Riding a bus, I gave up my seat to an older woman. Almost immediately, another person gave up his seat for me. It seemed okay for an aging woman of 80 to stand in a bus; but having a foreigner stand was unacceptable.

What do the Chinese envy about America? They envy our beautiful country. They admire our beautiful flag. They admire our world-class education system. They wholeheartedly admire our first-rate, strong and competent military.

They admire our individuality. They admire our unrestrictive access to freedom. They admire our ability to live in and purchase huge homes, monster trucks and other excesses. They envy our self-confidence, our Rolex watches, and our propensity to be overweight. Who wouldn't want to be an American?

What puzzles the Chinese about Americans? The average Chinese cannot comprehend our fascination with guns. With the carnage on our streets the Chinese see this as a simple. *Ban guns.*

One thing that Americans fail to realize, when bands of bearded citizens brandishing assault rifles in public, that is seen here. When a mob storms our capital, it is headline news in China. When a president openly mocks others and

46

incites violence, the world sees that. *Is this a summation of democracy?*

Would I live here forever? The topic has come up. Their medical system is good. Their dentists are excellent. The government is responsive and efficient. Living expenses are minimal. Restaurants are varied, and the food is "worthy."

China possesses a mass transit system unsurpassed. While the rest of the world wrestled with the pandemic, China in three months had it contained.

The Strength of China is its people.

One faculty member brought his wife and seven children over with him. His wife was somewhat concerned about the language barrier. Every evening, she walked around the university oval running track across from the apartments where she lived. In the evening, a number of those residents would also run or walk on that same track.

A Chinese lady, similar in age, was concerned about this American walking alone and walked with her. Communicating through their smartphones, they coordinated their schedules so that they could walk and talk with each other.

Over time, the two families did things socially together. When the pandemic hit, the same Chinese lady would go shopping for this American family, concerned about their welfare.

As a postscript to this article, my wife and I were caught between semesters in the United States when the pandemic hit. We taught remotely (as most professors did) that Spring semester from our townhouse in Fort Worth, Texas. Receiving special permission to return, we came back in September, after taking three Covid tests. As we arrived entering the Shanghai Pudong Airport, we were isolated and quarantined for 14-days. Towards the end, we were climbing the walls, but were safe. The precautions taken by the Chinese seemed extreme and overkill, *and we were glad of it.*

47

From Afterthought to Forethought: How a Design Program Shifted

CHLOE IRLA

Assistant Professor of Art,
McDaniel College,
Westminster, Maryland, USA

Keywords

design education, design curriculum,
instructional design, introduction
to design, foundations, curriculum
design

THE RISKS AND REWARDS OF ADJUSTING A CURRICULUM

In 2018, my institution went through an existential crisis. So did my academic department, which was then called *Art & Art History*. Now, we're just *Art*. My pedagogical responsibilities shifted that year. In 2016, I was hired as an Assistant Professor of Art and taught new courses called Art & Digital Culture and New Media Art that allowed students to experiment with making art on a computer. After only three years, those two classes are no longer offered as I'm now responsible for teaching existing graphic design courses.

I'm an alumnus of my institution and transferred there as a junior from a prominent art college in the early 2000's. The Art & Art History department has always been small and in 2016 consisted of two tenured or tenure-track Art faculty (myself included), three tenured or tenure-track Art Historians, one lecturer, and seven adjunct faculty members. Students then and now choose between two specializations within the Art major: Studio Art or Graphic Design (2020). In 2005, the two required graphic design courses, Graphic Design I and Graphic Design II, went from being taught by a since-retired full Professor to being taught by a series of adjunct instructors who worked full-time jobs as designers. These instructors were absolutely qualified to teach the courses and had the professional experience that was worth modeling to students. But one cannot and should not expect an instructor, who already has a full-time job and is only making $3000 per class, to have the bandwidth to deeply connect with cohorts of students.

Results from a department-sponsored survey that went out to Art students and alumni in 2015 showed that students were unhappy with the rotating cast of contingent faculty teaching graphic design. Our students want jobs after graduating and need reliable mentorship to help them achieve their goals. When I joined the institution as a faculty member in 2016, I inherited the responsibility of advising the required student graphic design internships. I wasn't expected to teach Graphic Design I or II and was encouraged to develop my own new classes. It was stressful to develop a curriculum without knowing what students were learning in these existing graphic design classes. My colleagues and I began to notice a problem with the structure and timing of our curriculum. Graphic Design specialization students took their required foundation courses (Perceptual Drawing and 2D Design Concepts) from adjunct instructors during their first or second year. Students then took Graphic Design I and II from adjunct instructors during their junior year. During Junior Reviews, an annual voluntary critique of students' work to help advise them on future courses to take, full-time Art faculty would often be meeting Graphic Design specialization students for the first time. When asked, students couldn't name a single living graphic designer. Student work wasn't showing technical competencies. I knew that changes needed to be made and began a crusade to establish graphic design as a robust part of our curriculum.

It was somewhat serendipitous that our institution went through a significant faculty-led program evaluation in 2018 (Jaschik,

48

2019). Each department had to produce a set of materials that essentially justified its existence, including how many students were in the major pipeline, the numbers of students enrolled in each class dating back five years, and the successes of alumni. It was also a chance for each department to dream big and pitch new ideas to help boost enrollment within the discipline. Each department compiled their information in a report and sent it to a select committee of faculty members called the Strategic Thinking Group on Pedagogical Value. At the conclusion of this process, the STGPV, Provost, and President would inform each major whether it was going to be invested in, not changed at all, restructured, or deactivated.

As an Assistant Professor, I took a risk and disagreed with my department chair's vision for the future. That vision included a focus on expanding Studio Art and hiring a full-time sculptor. I thought that this ignored what current and prospective students wanted, which was an investment in graphic design. Students had to take Drawing I and 2D Design Concepts before they could take Graphic Design I. These pre-requisites were a barrier to the growth of our program, as Graphic Design I typically enrolled no more than eight students each year. In my opinion, these pre-requisites weren't serving the department. We needed to find a way to teach Graphic Design I that could accommodate any student and fit within a broader curriculum beyond a singular focus on Art. My chair felt that there was no way that graphic design could be taught to students who didn't already know how to draw. As an Assistant Professor, this disagreement put me in an uncomfortable situation. Our department's report was limited to a specific length and I didn't feel as though my contributions were fully included in our submission. I discretely emailed a separate proposal focused on graphic design to the STGPV, who had previously communicated that they were open to receiving supplemental ideas outside of departmental reports. I felt like I was betraying my department chair, who's the only tenured Art faculty member at my institution. But the future of our program was on the line and the last thing that I wanted was for the Art major to be deactivated.

This proved to be a risk worth taking as two

months later, we received a response from the STGPV that Art was going to be invested in, with a focus on building the graphic design specialization. The news was bittersweet. While Art would be invested in, the Art History major within our department would be deactivated. With one colleague already retiring, this meant that one of the remaining two Art Historians would have to leave the college. It felt like Art's investment was at the expense of Art History's. Through this process, my institution deactivated five majors overall: Art History, Religious Studies, Music, German, and French.

The program evaluation made it clear that the institution's investment in Art, including the addition of future full-time faculty members, would correlate directly with the number of students who signed up to be majors. Change wasn't going to happen overnight. During my department's follow-up meeting with the President and the Provost, it was decided that the best course of action for our students and for the livelihood of our department would be for me to take over teaching the existing graphic design courses. The pre-requisites for Graphic Design I needed to be removed to increase enrollment and the pre-requisites for Graphic Design II would be adjusted to ensure that students were entering that class with both technical and conceptual knowledge.

Design is not siloed from Art yet in small programs like ours, the competition for majors between and within departments is cutthroat and divisive. As a generalist with a liberal arts background myself, I have mixed feelings about developing classes and programs solely intended to get students jobs after graduation. I don't believe that teaching students to use the Adobe software just so that they can get a desk job and make money for somebody else is the right direction to take. I'd rather introduce students to technical skills, conceptual foundations, the importance of collaboration, and creative thinking strategies that they can use to empower themselves in the future, whether they want to become designers or not. I saw the potential for Graphic Design I to be included in other major and minor programs at our institution, such as Marketing, Entrepreneurship, Writing & Publishing, and Communication. When I adopted the Graphic Design I and Graphic

49

Graphic Design I course description, 2005-2019:

A studio activity stressing the importance of the imaginative and creative talents of the artist in today's commercial art world.

Graphic Design I course description, 2020-present:

This studio course serves as an introduction to the professional scope and creative field of graphic design. Students will be introduced to the basics of visual communication including typography and image creation through projects that stress learning various design tools and conceptual development.

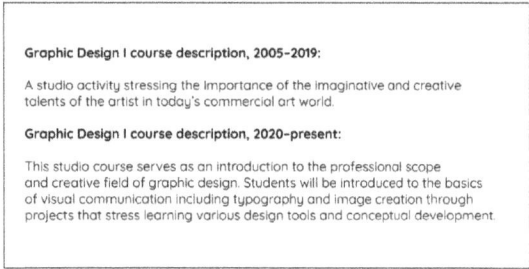

Figure 1: Past and present graphic design course descriptions from institutional academic catalogs dated 2017 and 2020. (Source: Courses). Image by C. Irla.

Design II courses, I rewrote their descriptions to better fit a contemporary introduction to design (See figure 1). I wanted these courses to exemplify Michael Bierut's quote, "The great thing about design is that it is almost always about something else" (Bierut, 2006).

In 2019, the aftermath of our program's evaluation was tense as our department was emotional about the loss of the Art History major and a departed colleague. After several meetings that included presenting research that I conducted on

over one hundred institutions that offer graphic design, my chair agreed to drop the pre-requisites to Graphic Design I. I added a general education "tag" that would make the course more attractive to non-majors needing to fulfill a graduation requirement. My chair and I worked together to update the Graphic Design Specialization within the Art major. We added existing courses that would guarantee that every student in the major pipeline would interface with a full-time faculty member in the department within their first two years of study (See figure 2). Through lobbying and collaboration with other colleagues on campus, Graphic Design I became a part of the Marketing minor, Entrepreneurship minor, and Sports Marketing major. Graphic Design I would be offered every semester instead of once per year while Graphic Design II would be offered every Spring. Upon course registration for fall 2020, 14 of 18 available seats filled. In 2019, Graphic Design I enrolled a total of eight students. In that one registration period, we almost doubled the class's enrollment from the previous year.

Art-Graphic Design Specialization

OLD

Required Courses:

History of Western Art I
History of Western Art II
A History of Modern Art

Perceptual Drawing or
First-Year Seminar - Mark to Message: Drawing Now

2D Design
Graphic Design I
Graphic Design II
Four-credit graphic design internship
Capstone: Senior Show Preparation

Choose two courses:

Principles of Marketing
Introduction to Communication: Media
Professional Communication
Introduction to Psychology

Three Studio Art courses

UPDATED

Required Foundation Courses:

Perceptual Drawing
2D Design Concepts
Art as Work
3D Design Concepts
Digital Imaging

Required Courses:

History of Western Art I
History of Western Art II
A History of Modern Art
Graphic Design I
Graphic Design II
Four-credit graphic design internship
Capstone: Exhibition/Professional Practice

Choose one courses:

Basic Video Editing
Audio Production
Digital Publishing
Scenic and Properties Design

Two Art Elective Courses

Figure 2: Previous and current Art major with a specialization in Graphic Design curriculum (Courses). Image by C. Irla.

50

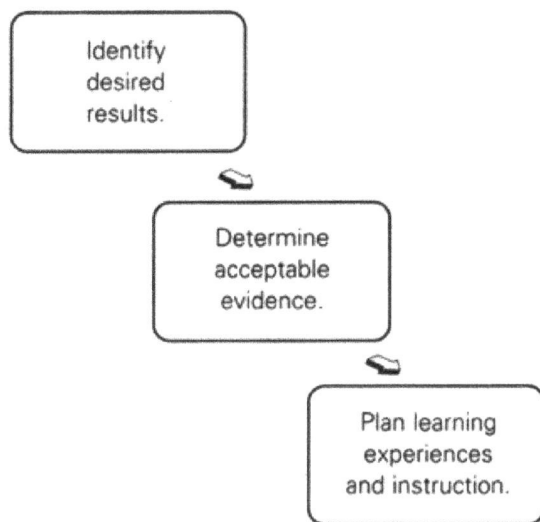

Figure 3: Stages in the Backward Design Process
(Source: Wiggins & McTighe, 1998)

I spent summer 2020 developing the Graphic Design I course. In 2018, I took a class at my institution called *Principles of Redesign for Hybrid & Blended Learning.* I was introduced to instructional design and best practices for hybrid and online teaching. When designing a new course, there's an element of user experience design in that it is in the best interest of instructors to put themselves in the position of each learner in the class. I utilized a backwards design model to first establish the course's learning outcomes and then built my assignments and content around those objectives (See figure 3). The course needed to be broad yet concise, challenging yet fun. It needed to balance the introduction of technical skills on a computer with conceptual foundations. It also needed to introduce graphic design as a multidisciplinary, socially-engaged field. There was a lot of ground to cover.

The final outcome of the course would be a portfolio book that students would have printed at the end of the semester. The content of the book would be generated throughout the semester and showcase projects and writings by the student. I divided up the course into six units: Introduction to Typography, Graphic Design is CRAP (Contrast, Repetition, Alignment, Proximity), Expressive Typography, Promotion & Engagement, Holiday Greetings, and Final Portfolio Development. The content of the course includes video tutorials that I made specifically for each project, software tutorials provided by Hoonuit Learning, online lectures and videos

such as *How Posters Work* by Ellen Lupton, and readings from *GO: A Kidd's Guide to Graphic Design* by Chip Kidd, *The Non-Designer's Design Book* by Robin Williams, *Thinking with Type* by Ellen Lupton, *Graphic Design: The New Basics* by Ellen Lupton and Jennifer Cole Phillips, and *The Elements of Typographic Style* by Robert Bringhurst. The course materials and content are carefully curated to fit each unit's objectives.

The first part of each unit introduces theory and content–*why are we doing this project?* (See figure 4) The content is reiterated through in-class activities that do not take place on a computer. For example, in our Promotion & Engagement unit, students design and draw a lost pet-style poster for our beloved college mascot. Designing by hand before introducing digital tools forces the student to correlate the analog and digital realms. They better understand the purpose and ease of using a grid in InDesign, for example, if they had to draw their own by hand using a straightedge and a pencil during the in-class activity. The activity helps to make the content stick. The second part of each unit focuses on practice–*how are we doing this project?* Students have dedicated work time during each class period to apply what they learned from the software tutorials and seek help. Students meet in groups to share their progress and get feedback. When a project is turned in, the first submission doesn't count towards the final grade. The student will receive thorough verbal feedback from me and then apply edits to their work before submitting the final version at the end of the semester. This method teaches students that designing is an iterative process based on feedback rather than a letter grade.

The syllabus states that "this course serves as an introduction to the creative and professional realm of graphic design." It skims the surface to get students engaged. Each module brief, visual examples, readings, and software tutorials are dots that the student must connect to create the deliverables. Briefs from fictitious clients are utilized to introduce each project and inform students of important deadlines, learning objectives, technical procedures and requirements, and deliverables. Attaching a client to each project forces the student to make decisions based on someone else's needs. Supplemental documents support each brief and include visual

51

	Meeting Day 1	Meeting Day 2
Week 1 (Theory)	Introduce content and the module brief	In-class activity to support the content
Week 2 (Practice)	In-class work time	In-class work time + feedback from classmates

Figure 4: Face-to-face classroom meeting structure. Image by C. Irla.

examples that provide a thorough overview of past and present designers from diverse backgrounds. Representation matters. With 36.3% of our institution's undergraduates identifying as Domestic Students of Color (2020), it's a disservice to all to only amplify one style of work or demographic.

By the third unit of the semester, students have developed some technical competency in Photoshop and InDesign and have completed two projects about the basics of typography. The third project, *Expressive Typography: Dreams*, reiterates the importance of form and content as students are tasked with transforming a dimensional, physical artwork into a digital installation. Students are introduced to design projects that are sculptural, material-oriented, and installed in physical spaces like Nari Ward's *We The People* installation composed of shoelaces from 2011 (See figure 5).

The client for this project is a fictitious Dean of Outreach and Community Engagement at our institution who wants dimensional,

Figure 5: *We The People* by Nari Ward, 2011. Image from 2012 (Ward, 2012)

typographical installations located around campus. The installations should be based on the designer's interpretation of two Langston Hughes poems, *Harlem* and *Dreams*. The Dean would like for the materials used in the installations to relate to the content and its message. The typography should be based on a slab serif, decorative, blackletter, or script typeface that reinforces the importance of maintaining hopes and dreams amidst uncertainty. Before being permanently installed, designers must submit mockups of their installations. These mockups will be considered for approval and funding by the Dean and a committee of staff members. Not only do students have to research the poems and create their work (see figures 6–8), but they also have to write persuasively to pitch their ideas and explain their design choices.

The feedback that I received from students in my course evaluations proved that they enjoyed the structure of the course and were challenged while learning. One student commented, "I think the strongest part of the course was the way everything was laid out. It was so clear what we needed to do and when." Another stated, "The breadth of instructional content provided was awesome! To access not only video tutorials recorded by yourself [the instructor], but also professional Adobe tutorials and other content via YouTube was very helpful in my learning. It kept things fresh and the content was never boring or repetitive. Also the assignments themselves were so much fun. Each assignment was original and unlike anything I've done in the several previous graphic design courses I've taken dating back to high school. Course was very

52

well organized and elements were clearly labeled. Work load was challenging but not too heavy."

With the implementation of new pre-requisites for Graphic Design II, eight students enrolled for the course in spring 2021, up from five students in spring 2020. Registration for my Graphic Design I class in spring 2021 confirmed that the course was in high demand, as 22 students enrolled with 12 students on the waitlist. I worked with my department chair to hire and train an adjunct instructor to teach a second section of Graphic Design I. For me, the enrollment growth inspires a sense of accomplishment — my intuition about what students wanted was correct — but will these numbers yield new Art majors? I don't know. Starting this year, my institution has a new President, Provost, and Vice President of Finance and the prospect of another faculty-led program evaluation is possible. For now, I embrace a future where more students at our liberal arts institution are exposed to design and encouraged to incorporate that knowledge into their other areas of interest.

REFERENCES

Bierut, M. (2006, March 18). *Warning: May Contain Non-Design Content*. Design Observer. https://designobserver.com/feature/warning-may-contain-non-design-content/4137.

Courses. Courses - McDaniel College - Acalog ACMS™. (n.d.). http://catalog.mcdaniel.edu/content.php?catoid=33&navoid=2191.

Courses. Courses - McDaniel College - Acalog ACMS™. (n.d.). http://catalog.mcdaniel.edu/content.php?catoid=44&navoid=2916.

Jaschik, S. (2019, February 25). *McDaniel College Eliminates 5 Majors and 3 Minors*. Inside Higher Ed.https://www.insidehighered.com/quicktakes/2019/02/25/mcdaniel-college-eliminates-5-majors-and-3-minors

McDaniel College. (2020). *A College That Will Change Your Life*. Fast Facts & Accolades. https://www.mcdaniel.edu/about-us/fast-facts-accolades.

McDaniel College. (2020). Art. https://www.mcdaniel.edu/academics/departments/art-department/art.

Ward, N. (2012). *We the People*. https://library-artstor-org.hoover2.mcdaniel.edu:2443/asset/AWSS35953_35953_35427617. Artstor.

Wiggins, G., & McTighe, J. (1998). *Stages in the Backward Design Process*. Understanding by Design. Association for Supervision and Curriculum Development. https://educationaltechnology.net/wp-content/uploads/2016/01/backward-design.pdf.

Figure 6: With his artwork digitally installed on the backside of the gymnasium, Jordan Davis used shoelaces and Nike Air Max 90's to encourage students to chase their dreams.

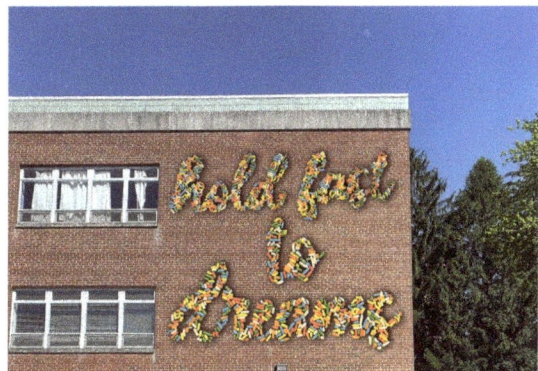

Figure 7: Kaylen Buschhorn used sprinkles to inspire students with this cheerful digital installation across from campus housing.

Figure 8: In her digital installation, Leah Wilder used yarn fragments to inspire student-athletes who play on the nearby athletic fields.

53

Long Papers

SHIFT →

Creating through Crisis: *First Things First, Revisited (Again)*

DANIELLE FOUSHEE

Arizona State University
Arizona, USA

Keywords
First Things First, Covid-19, justice,
social impact, community, capitalism

Since the 1964 publication of the original First Things *First Manifesto* (Garland et al.), many designers have lamented the pull of consumer capitalism on the design professions. Practitioners can be lured by money, power, and "rock star" status, most commonly in service to commercial interests that evangelize a culture of insatiable desire for *more stuff*. In 1999, a new cohort of signatories republished the manifesto for the new millennium, claiming that things had gotten worse, not better. They advocated for a new generation of designers to address the same social and cultural

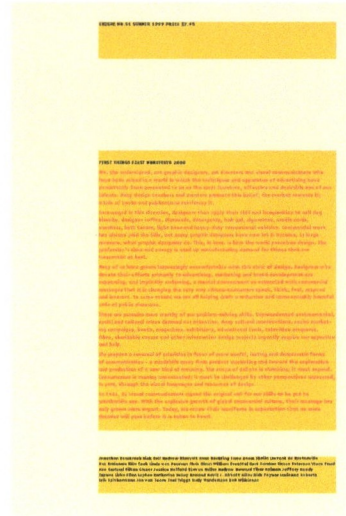

Figure 1: First Things First Manifesto 2000. Emigre #51 [cover].

demands made 36 years earlier (Barnbrook, et al.). Now, the design community is called on *again* to meet the urgency of our time. Consumer culture can no longer distract us from our purpose. We are obligated to reorient our attention to research, creative practices, and pedagogies that serve the people around us; repair our social, cultural, and political systems; and heal the Earth itself.

The year 2020 brought a convergence of challenges that "design thinkers" like to call *wicked problems*. The world was infected by the Covid-19 pandemic. Most of us stayed home, quarantined ourselves, and built safe cocoons (unless we were so-called "essential workers"[1]). In the United States, we continue to console our friends and families as more than 600,000 people have died, so far. The global death toll recently tallied over 4 million (Cunningham, 2021). We watched in disbelief as many of our fellow citizens refused to come together to care for one another. We also watched in awe as individual healthcare workers risked their own lives to make sure we survived.

Figure 2: Mindmap documenting how design practice, education, and research is implicated and impacted by Covid-19, Black Lives Matter, politics, and the economy in 2020.

---

1 Eyeroll.

If we didn't experience job losses personally, most of us sympathized with the millions of Americans who were driven deeper into poverty as lockdowns lingered. We looked on helplessly as many of our elected government officials ignored the will of the country's people, subverted its democratic system, and incited a seditious insurrection on our Capitol. We witnessed in horror as our Black community members were attacked and killed by police officers — sparking worldwide protests against systemic racism. Vast swaths of the country burned as wildfires destroyed towns and homes across California, Oregon, Colorado, and Arizona.[2] In every aspect of our lives, designers have made choices that contributed to these outcomes.

As the year dragged on, the onslaught of outrage compounded day after day. "To some extent," predicted Garland (1964), "[designers] are all helping draft a reductive and immeasurably harmful code of public discourse." We contribute to this discourse by creating artifacts and telling stories that, in either overt or covert ways, uphold imperial power structures.[3] In our hyper-competitive capitalist culture, real people are objectified and homogenized as lifeless "consumers." They're guided [with the help of designers] to see the world through a lens of scarcity. It's no wonder so many people are compelled to spend more and more money in their quest for fulfillment. In fact, the average American household now holds more than $145,000 in debt (Fay, 2021). Stephen Satterfield, food writer and host of the recent documentary film *High on the Hog: How African Cuisine Transformed America*, talks about the ways in which our humanity has been lost in the current hegemonic system: "The only way we know how to express empathy and care is to buy stuff, give [people] money. [For example, a] woman is slaughtered. Start a Go-Fund-Me for the family. It's like we don't know how to give care" (Braswell, 2021). We shouldn't be surprised; after all, our lives seem to revolve around money.

Fifty-four years ago (just 3 years after the initial publication of *First Things First*), Guy Debord's

---

2 As a district ranger in the U.S. Forest Service, my husband works every summer on wildfire teams across the western states. As of this writing in June 2021, there are more than 20 fires burning across Arizona's landscape. They've had to ration resources for fire-fighting because there are not enough personnel to go around.

3 According to critical theorists Althusser (1971) and Foucault (1976), there are two systems of power that command broad-scale social conformity: one is corporeal, and the other is ideological. Designers most often create products that affirm the ideologies of the dominant culture including: patriarchy, individualism, competition, growth, and property ownership, among others.

tamarawebb_ #mindset:
I'm so thankful for all the people who said no to me. To all the people who told me I would never succeed and laugh at my goals and passion.

They made me want to achieve happiness in what I do even MORE ♥

_____

In Dubai with @vogueeyewear. An experience I will surely never forget! Stay tuned for more adventures 😍♥ 🦇

#showyourVogue
#VogueEyewear MT 😎
#VogueSquad

♡ ◯ ↑   ⬚

Liked by iggyfenech and 2,750 others

6 DAYS AGO

Figure 3: @tamarawebb on Instagram.

(1967/1994) *Society of the Spectacle* forecast a cultural transformation that values appearances over reality — images over people. Social media brings this warning to fruition as we are (implicitly and explicitly) urged to aestheticize ourselves into objects of perfection. The "personal branding" phenomenon turns individual people into commodities, or "influencers" — human objects to be bought and sold for profit. Influencers like @tamarawebb (figure 3) typically share images of themselves (almost always alone) modeling or using branded products in some luxurious or exotic location. Viewers are persuaded to buy these products as surrogates for the transformational experiences they long for.[4] Famously, industrial design professor Victor Papanek (1971) lamented the toxic partnership between design and consumer capitalism when he said:

> Design has satisfied only evanescent wants and desires, while the genuine needs of man have often been neglected by the designer. The economic, psychological, spiritual, technological, and intellectual needs of a human being are usually more difficult and less profitable to satisfy than the carefully engineered and manipulated 'wants' inculcated by fad and fashion. (p. 15)

And, when audiences never see the destructive machinery that works behind the scenes, they are blinded to the ways capitalist systems prey on young, solo entrepreneurs until they burn out and disappear. One influencer said (Swanson, 2021),

> I feel like I'm a walking museum, bro . . . The scary thing is you never know how long this is going to last. That's what eats a lot of us at night. It's like, What's next? How long can we entertain everyone for? How long before no one cares, and what if your life was worth nothing?

Another regretted having gotten involved at all (Jennings, 2020);

> It's scary because it's this spiral of not ever feeling like you're enough, and that leaves this mental scarring. It's contributed to my mental health not being the best lately. I definitely had to get some therapy because of this.

Indeed, runaway market competition feeds on our natural insecurities and faces few consequences after real people's lives have been ruined.

Our economic system was intentionally designed to yield maximum ecological extraction, maximum production, maximum efficiency, and maximum profit in industries including agriculture, manufacturing, distribution, and healthcare — all of which collapsed at once under the weight of the uncontrolled global pandemic. Now, more than a year into the crisis, some resources remain hard to access,[5] and people of color have suffered the most.[6] When we couldn't get toilet paper, cleaning supplies, basic food items, or a simple medical test, we became acutely aware of the flaws inherent in designing for the singular outcome of profit-making.

Designers talk about empathy all the time, but often fail to follow through. Instead of addressing real social and environmental needs, so-called "innovators" like Amazon, Facebook, and Google prioritize "user experience design" insofar as it will bring in more and more cash.[7] For example, Amazon's corporate mission states, "Amazon strives to be Earth's Most Customer-Centric Company" (Amazon, n.d.), and it's now larger than its ten biggest competitors combined (Neufeld, 2020). In 2020 — during the height of the Covid-19 pandemic — the company's sales soared an additional 70% over the previous year (Amazon, 2020). And Amazon's founder Jeff Bezos' personal fortune increased by $74 *billion* (Bloomberg, 2021). Clearly, designers have created an enviable customer experience, but their empathy doesn't seem to extend to the company's 1.3 million employees who are treated with outright hostility. According to Forbes, Amazon's warehouse employees are seriously

---

4 A 2019 Morning Consult study reported that 88% of Gen Z and Millennials learn about products they want to buy on social media.

5 In May 2021, CNN reported continued shortages of a range of products including chicken, chlorine, gas, ketchup, lumber, metals, and steel.

6 According to the American Hospital Association (2020), in the early months of the pandemic, Black Chicagoans accounted for 72% of its positive Covid-19 cases despite making up only 32% of the city's total population. Another study in California revealed that Black Americans were 2.7 times more likely to be hospitalized than their White counterparts (Sutter Health, 2020).

7 Only after a violent mob stormed the U.S. Capital and threatened elected officials' physical safety on January 6, 2021, did powerful corporate interests and social media companies finally take action against fake news and incitement of violence. According to a study by Zignal Labs, online misinformation dropped by 73%, and the use of capitol riot hashtags plunged by 95% after former President Trump was banned from social media sites (Ghosh, 2021).

58

injured on the job 80% more often than their counterparts doing comparable work for other companies (McCarthy, 2021). Delivery drivers have been groaning for years about Amazon's unreasonable productivity targets that force them to save time by urinating in bottles. A driver in Detroit said, "It's inhumane, to say the least" (Taylor and Hartmans, 2021). These indignities, combined with the amalgamation of crises over the past year have ignited a sudden and profound transformation of personal and social values across the global West.

Designers, like so many others, have long served a malignant system that abuses our humanity and wrecks the environment. Most of us have been distracted from and oblivious to the social and physical well-being of our communities and their members. But, the pandemic offered time and space to reflect — to reconsider what we need and want from our lives and relationships. In the U.S. and around the world, our sense of community is shifting, our ideas of success are changing, and we're reevaluating our life's purposes. According to the most recent Edelman Trust Barometers (2020, 2021), 56% of people worldwide now believe that capitalism does more harm than good, and 64% say that they want to see positive social change in how we live, work, and treat one another. Ethical designers will pay attention to these changes and will make meaningful efforts to reorient our "priorities in favour of more useful, lasting, and democratic forms of communication — a mindshift away from product marketing and toward the exploration of a new kind of meaning...Consumerism...must be challenged by other perspectives..." (Garland, et. al., 1964). Today, everyday citizens are taking matters into their own hands — designing a world where they want to live. In response to multiple and ongoing existential crises, people are beginning to prioritize hyper-local engagement.

Without much help from professional designers, a diverse coalition of citizens reignited the fight against systemic forms of oppression at the local level. At the same time, thrift has become essential — even aspirational — during lockdowns, quarantine, and beyond. And mutual aid efforts, community gardens, and resource sharing are being normalized as people are re-engaging with others in in-person relationships closer to home. These values are already coming

to life through grassroots design practices that leverage existing community assets — human and not — to make change. Jeremy Myerson (2016), design faculty at the Royal College of Art, suggests that we work against business models that prioritize growth and instead, focus our attention on "scaling down." Still widely accepted as a key to success, "scaling up" is a remnant of old industrial-era thinking. The objective was to maximize growth and profit by implementing a singular design solution that, in theory, served everyone efficiently and universally. While these ambitions may have been well-intentioned, we now know that designing with local needs and cultural specificity in mind is more beneficial and sustainable than a one-size-fits-all approach.

Designers are uniquely equipped to help organize, develop, and create conditions that can both remove barriers and ease transitions to a new social and cultural paradigm that puts well-being above the machinations of unsustainable economic growth. Our design students are eager to work toward these changes. At Arizona State University, the majority of my students choose to explore ways in which designers should (1) **demand work-life balance**, (2) **reverse environmental degradation**, and (3) **fight for social justice**. Samantha Hillenburg, a senior in ASU's graphic design program reflected:

> [Most of us] can agree that [designers] have the ability to contour reality, bring communities together, and control the narrative. My biggest inspiration for design is its ability to speak. Design has the biggest voice in today's society and we need to use it for good in what matters: social inequity, political injustice, and climate change issues. Our world is more globalized than ever and designers have the responsibility to be involved with social and cultural issues (2021).

While my observations are limited to design students at Arizona State University, their experiences and attitudes are not isolated. Their ideas mirror the larger cultural changes in mindset that were accelerated by Covid-19. I encourage them to look inward to discover what matters deeply to them, I support and acknowledge the truth of their feelings, and I help them articulate and stand in their convictions with confidence. Despite the discomfort we sometimes experience through this

59

process, they have a safe space to find their voices and to practice using them.

WORK/LIFE BALANCE

Covid-19 forced everyone to slow down and stay home, and lots of folks realized that our typical American "always busy" lifestyle had never contributed much to our quality of life in the first place. During lockdowns, many of us spent more time with our families, reconnected with personal passions, developed new hobbies, and connected with neighbors. We reengaged with our domestic lives through home-cooking, gardening, and DIY projects. In light of these trends, I asked my graduate students to conduct a self-study as a way to process the many layers of change they were experiencing in relation to their personal values and goals. They worked on life/career manifestos, and their work espouses strong values of family, community, beauty, and purpose. Aubri Blueeyes lost a number of her family members due to Covid-19, which gave her pause to rethink her heritage, her priorities, and her future. She writes,

> I have been raised almost all my life on the Navajo reservation in New Mexico. My family and their families before them have always lived on the reservation we call home. We are tied and connected to it. My grandparents tell me stories about their relatives that also lived on the land. As for me, I am born into the Red House Clan — my mother's clan — that was passed down to me. It is my culture, tradition, and identity. I will eventually pass this down to my children and then thereafter. However, [after leaving home for several years] I have found that I am losing a part of who I am as a person. My manifesto is not only an embodiment of me but also an embodiment of my traditions and values. Through it, I will reconnect with my language and culture as well as with the land (2020).

Indeed, many of us are trying to avoid jumping back into our old habits. "I think the pandemic has changed my mindset in a way, like I really value my time now," said 27-year old software developer Jonathan Caballero (Hsu, 2021).

As people looked for ways to reduce their Covid stress and isolation, "Zoom towns" popped up across the country in exurban and rural areas, especially when opportunities to work-from-home offered employees more freedom and flexibility to live anywhere. Now, many of us are not willing to go back: 40% say they would quit if they had to return to the office (Melin and Egkolfopoulou, 2021). College students also appreciate the flexibility of working from anywhere. Due to Covid, some college students dropped out or took a gap year rather than attend school online. But many more persevered — and 73% now say they hope at least some of their courses remain online post-pandemic (McKenzie, 2021). Anecdotally, students in both my studio and seminar courses were more focused and achieved better outcomes after the university transitioned to online learning. Most of them were less distracted, more engaged with their group work, more thoughtful, and their contributions in class discussions on Slack were more robust. Plus, introverts increased their overall class participation. I also heard from a number of students that they built relationships online with classmates they rarely talked to when they were all physically in the same rooms together on campus.

Now, officials are beginning the slow process of easing Covid-19 restrictions;[8] restaurants and businesses are starting to reopen; schools are planning their return to in-person learning, and social life is rebounding. Jobs are plentiful again. Before the pandemic, Americans likely tied our sense of self to our work. But after more than a year of uncertainty and instability, many of us discovered that incessant workaholism had never been satisfying or fulfilling. Four million Americans quit their jobs in April alone (U.S. Bureau of Labor Statistics, 2021). We're also less willing to endure exploitative treatment by our employers. A food-service worker in Galveston, Texas said, "It's not okay to risk your employees' lives over someone's cheeseburger" (Vinopal, 2021).

As Covid begins to recede, many of us are choosing a different path forward — reserving our time for things that make us happier and healthier. Tennis superstar Naomi Osaka set

---

8 The pandemic is still raging in some parts of the world and resurging in others, and in June the World Health Organization recommended that even vaccinated people continue taking precautions due to the more dangerous Delta variant of the virus (Rabin, Mandavilli, and Hubler, 2021).

60

a great example when she dropped out of the French Open rather than submit to critical and demeaning interactions with the press. She told officials she was protecting her mental health (Crouse, 2021). And she's not alone. One group of design students at ASU came together this spring to protest what they believed were unreasonable assignment timelines and a toxic learning environment. To support their demands, the cohort shared personal stories of the negative mental and physical health impacts they attributed to the learning culture. Writing for my design rhetoric course, one student shared his experience:

> The taxing nature of the [ASU undergrad-uate design] program's workload can cause students to act out of desperation just to keep up. I know from personal experience. During my first year in the program, I was prescribed methylphenidate to increase my focus, despite never showing a need for that medication during my childhood. The medication felt helpful because I was staying focused longer and getting more done. It made work more stimulating for me, which helps when you have to maintain focus for 10 hours a day. But I couldn't tell how stimulated I was supposed to feel and I didn't have the time to figure that out with my doctor because of the demands of school. Eventually I stopped taking the medication because I wanted to know that I could keep up in school without getting high. Ever since this experience I have been plagued by self-doubt (Anonymous, 2021).

The students also conducted a localized survey and found that most of their classmates focused on school work for about 50 hours per week, plus spent 20 hours at their part-time jobs. After suffering through the upheaval of their lives and future uncertainty, they're no longer willing to accept this arrangement. They also complained about pro-bono class projects they're required to do for real-world clients without compensation, as well as an atmosphere that — to them — seems to pit students against one another in fierce competition. Instead, they say they want a supportive culture that values their hard work and prizes sharing, collaboration, and community. I'm doing everything I can to help them achieve these goals.

CLIMATE CHANGE

Covid-19 and other recent natural disasters are making the existential dangers posed by climate change unavoidable. This summer, an unprecedented heat wave in the Pacific Northwest and Canada crushed previous records; on June 29, 2021, Lytton, Canada hit 121°![9] The following day, an uncontrolled wildfire burned down the whole town (McGrath, 2021). The National Interagency Coordination Center (2021), which collects data about wildfires across the U.S. reported that in 2020, 59,000 ignitions occurred and 10.1 million acres were burned nationwide. The Weather Channel also noted that in the first half of 2021, the number of wildfires in the U.S. was *four thousand* more than in a normal year. While the heat wave descended and wildfires raged in the west, a high rise condominium building in Miami, Florida, collapsed — presumably killing most of the more than 150 residents who were trapped inside.[10] The exact cause of this disaster is still under investigation, but many experts (including U.S. Energy Secretary Jennifer Granholm) are speculating about the role played by the rise in sea levels associated with climate change (Boyle, 2021). Meanwhile, Detroit was underwater after it received seven inches of rain in one day, turning freeways into rivers, stranding motorists, and flooding thousands of homes. To add insult to injury, during the same week, a lobbyist for Exxon, an international fossil fuels corporation, was caught on video discussing unseemly strategies the company uses to scuttle government actions on climate change, including spreading disinformation and working through shell organizations to manipulate lawmakers and public perceptions (Brady, 2021).

Our students are inheriting this life or death crisis caused not by them, but by the generations who came before. They are alarmed, and several have used my design thinking project to explore possible solutions. Junior graphic design student Savaani Thigale pitched a comprehensive program to help people transition to a zero-waste way of life. Her research showed that Millennials and Gen Z are most likely to adopt lifestyle changes, so she targeted her concept to their needs and

61

---

9 118° is the hottest temperature on record for Las Vegas, NV (Current Results, 2021).

10 At the time of this writing, the recovery efforts are still underway.

motivations. First, she argued for a one-stop shop for no-waste living. It would be like Wal-Mart, with food, housewares, clothing, personal hygiene products, and more. But none of the products would produce the type of waste that typically goes into landfills. She also suggested that — to keep participants motivated — she would create an app where people could track their progress and compare it to their friends and others in the community. And finally, she proposed a marketing campaign to drive excitement about the program and entice people to sign up. Other students have proposed equally compelling interventions.

People worldwide are waking up to the climate disaster we face, and during the pandemic-induced economic recession we had more time and energy to devote to reducing our impacts on the environment. A study by IBM (2020) proclaimed, "Sustainability hits its tipping point," and revealed that at least 77% of consumers say they want products that are eco-friendly. Designers' work is located at the nexus of ideas and artifacts, so it's time we take responsibility for the things we put into the world.

Instead of approaching environmental issues from a 'crisis' perspective, some students advocate for public access to nature as part of a healthy lifestyle. Their research shows the importance of nature to our well-being; it lowers blood pressure, boosts the immune system, increases attention, and improves mental health — while also encouraging environmental advocacy (Robbins, 2020). One of my students predicted that there would be a heightened need and desire for people to socialize outdoors and in public places after Covid-restrictions ease. He wrote,

> We still live in a world affected by the coronavirus pandemic. We still carry the feeling of danger when leaving the house to do things that once felt ordinary. There is no escaping that we live in troubling times, but we do know that this will not be a way of life that lasts forever. Once the clouds depart, there will be a newfound appreciation for being with others, being in the outdoors, and experiencing nature (Evans, 2021).

He suggests that graphic designers will find new opportunities to accommodate people's desire for comfortable and navigable outdoor public spaces

Figure 4: Black History Month Mural Project, organized by Gizette Knight and Reality Dreams; Phoenix, Arizona.

by engaging in the field of environmental graphic design. Heather Murphy agrees. She works for the City of Phoenix Streets Department and told me that their April 2021 traffic data revealed a 27% increase in bicycling since the start of the pandemic. Pet adoptions also skyrocketed. Nearly half of all Americans got a new dog (Rover, 2021) and with it, new reasons to get outside and move around. Porch concerts, sidewalk birthday parties, and neighborhood movie nights in the park are just a few of the outdoor community-oriented activities that have brought people together safely over the past year.

SOCIAL JUSTICE

Social justice, equality, and democracy were driven to the forefront of our minds last year, as well. Beginning with the wide disparity in Covid-19 healthcare outcomes for people of color and the murder of George Floyd by police, a majority of Americans were forced to acknowledge our country's racist systems. Worldwide, people of all ethnicities protested racial injustice throughout the summer, despite the risk of catching the virus. The famous phrase "Black Lives Matter" was painted larger than life on roadways, and portraits of police-shooting victims were painted in the streets. In Phoenix, Arizona, activist Gizette Knight organized an event in which artists painted 28 portraits of 28 influential Black people for Black History Month in February 2021 (figure 4).

People also got organized to participate in political life; more Americans voted in the 2020 Presidential elections than in any other contest in U.S. history. Now, reactionary politicians across the country are advancing new legislation to deny voting rights to millions of citizens — especially people of color. Propaganda and misinformation about race, class, and U.S. history are widespread. People in power are attempting to silence journalists and scholars in a coordinated effort to erase historical narratives of slavery and racial oppression from the culture. Investigative journalist and Black professor Nikole Hannah-Jones, who won a MacArthur Genius Fellowship and a Pulitzer Prize for her work on *The New York Times* "1619 Project,"[11] was recently denied tenure by politically-appointed trustees of University of North Carolina. Only after a massive public relations fiasco did they reconsider their position (Wamsley, 2021). In Florida, the governor signed a new law that appears to undermine academic freedom; its goal is to survey all public university faculty and students about their political beliefs in order to "promote intellectual diversity" (Andrade, 2021). Systemic racism has been designed into U.S. institutions since the country's founding, and we must remain diligent in our fights for academic integrity; historical accuracy; and social justice and economic leveling.

Our design students have begun to articulate their desire and expectations for a more complex understanding of their discipline that addresses these issues. And, they are eager to use their work to foster social justice and equality in the field and throughout society. Every semester, some of my design rhetoric students choose to write their editorials about the lack of diverse representation in their design history classes. Many students across the country are still learning from the same design history textbook I used in the 1990s! And too often, they're still being trained to follow so-called "rules" invented by (mostly) white European men nearly a century ago. ASU Senior Ali Wolf writes (2020):

> When we focus on history from a Eurocentric point of view, many perspectives are left out. Students from marginalized communities are implicitly encouraged to conform in order to be taken seriously in their learning environments, which discourages them from pursuing further education and careers in

design fields. When students and professionals leave the industry, creative teams are less successful.[12]

Former Senior Vice President at R/GA (Sao Paulo and San Francisco) and Latina designer Paola Colombo (2017) agrees:

> Diversity is not just an HR topic, it's a reflection of culture which influences how we live, how we communicate, what we need, which... influences the work we do as agents between our clients and the people they want to reach. As an agency expected to deliver innovation, we cannot create innovative work if our teams are homogenous.

As faculty in design we must practice what we preach; get out of our comfort zones; learn about design scholarship and practices outside the frameworks we learned in school; nurture our increasingly diverse student populations; and serve the specific needs of the varied communities our work targets.

Race is not the only diversity, equity, and inclusion issue designers and design educators need to fully embrace. Social justice reform in design education must also respond to discrimination against people with differences in physical and neurological ability, gender, sexual orientation, age, and more. Writing about the importance of universal design, ASU graduate student Michelle Jiang (2020) concludes:

> Graphic design doesn't have to be limited to visuals. There are millions of people with disabilities in America alone, and many graphic designers rarely consider this demographic. Through research, we can improve our users' experiences by adding audio and tactile design... Graphic design should not be limited to visual communication. Our field should be renamed Communication Design, which requires us to create whole-body experiences that appeal to all the senses: sight, sound, touch, taste, and smell.

Some higher ed programs in graphic design have already taken Jiang's advice, changing the name of the discipline to include all kinds of communication. But this is only a first step

63

---

11 The 1619 Project is a series of reports on the ways in which legacies of slavery are still impacting the lives of Black Americans today.

12 Lightly edited for length and clarity.

toward social justice in design and beyond. We have to do more.

CONCLUSION

Our students are dissatisfied with the status quo, and we should be too. Design education has coasted on old, outdated paradigms for way too long. As educators, we are obligated to confront changes in cultural and social values as they emerge. Other disciplines like engineering, business, biodesign, and computer science have already begun to adopt design processes to meet their needs, because traditional design disciplines have not consistently met the demands of our changing physical, virtual, social, and cultural environments.

Covid-19 has accelerated changes that were already underway. Neoliberal capitalism has for many years exploited people for profit, exacerbated social and economic inequities, compromised our health and wellbeing, undermined civic cohesion, corroded public trust, and ravaged the planet. The environment is increasingly toxic, poisoning humans, animals, and plant-life alike. Natural disasters are becoming more frequent and more deadly. And we can trace these problems directly to decisions made by designers since the Western Enlightenment. If we are to remain relevant — and more importantly, regain our integrity — we must make demonstrable changes now. Design educators must lead the way.

REFERENCES

Althusser, L. (1971). Ideology and ideological state apparatuses (Notes towards an investigation). *Lenin and Philosophy and Other Essays by Louis Althusser* (B. Brewster, Trans.) (pp. 127–186). Monthly Review Press.

Amazon (2020, October 29). Amazon.com announces third quarter results. Retrieved December 27, 2020 from https://ir.aboutamazon.com/news-release/news-release-details/2020/Amazon-com-Announces-Third-Quarter-Results/default.aspx

Andrade, S. (2021, June 24). Chilling new Florida law will survey university students and faculty about their political beliefs. Slate. https://slate.com/technology/2021/06/florida-survey-university-students-faculty-political-beliefs.html

Azar, K.M.J., Shen, Z., Romanelli, R.J., Lockhart S.H., Smits, K., Robinson, S., Brown, S., and Pressman, A.R. (May 21, 2020). Disparities in outcomes among covid-19 patients in a large health care system in california. *Health Affairs*, 39(7). https://doi.org/10.1377/hlthaff.2020.00598

Barnbrook, J., Kalman, T., Lupton, E., McCoy, K., Poynor, R., Miller, A., Roberts, L., van Toorn, J., VanderLans, R., Wilkinson, B., Bell, N., Keedy, J., Licko, Z., Mevis, A., Howard, A., Helfand, J., Glaser, M., Blauvelt, A., Bockting, H., . . . Spiekermann, E. (1999). First things first manifesto 2000. *Émigré*, (51, cover).

Bloomberg (2021). Bloomberg billionaires index. Retrieved January 2, 2021 from https://www.bloomberg.com/billionaires/?sref=GzMobW41

Boyle, L. (2021, June 30). Energy secretary suggests climate crisis may have played a role in Miami condo collapse. Independent. https://www.independent.co.uk/climate-change/miami-building-collapse-sea-climate-b1875007.html

Brady, J. (2021, July 1). Exxon lobbyist caught on video talking about undermining Biden's climate push. National Public *Radio*. https://www.npr.org/2021/07/01/1012138741/exxon-lobbyist-caught-on-video-talks-about-undermining-bidens-climate-push

Braswell, P. [Host]. (2021, June 16). High on the Hog's Stephen Satterfield: The Power of Black Storytelling (no. 2:7) [Audio podcast episode]. In *Race at Work*. Harvard Business Review.

Bureau of Labor Statistics (2021, June 8). Job Openings and Labor Turnover Summary. https://www.bls.gov/news.release/jolts.nro.htm

CBPP, Center on Budget and Policy Priorities (2020, December 18). Tracking the Covid-19 recession's effects on food, housing, and employment hardships. https://www.cbpp.org/research/poverty-and-inequality/tracking-the-covid-19-recessions-effects-on-food-housing-and

Crouse, L. (2021, June 1). Naomi Osaka and the power of 'Nope.' *The New York Times*. https://www.nytimes.com/2021/06/01/opinion/naomi-osaka-french-open-tennis.html

Cunningham, E. (2021, July 8). WHO sounds alarm as global deaths top 4 million, delta spreads to 100 countries. *The Washington Post*. https://www.washingtonpost.com/world/2021/07/08/covid-19-global-updates-who-sounds-alarm-global-deaths-top-4-million-delta-spreads-100-countries/

Current Results (2021). Weather Extremes. https://www.currentresults.com/Weather-Extremes/index.php

Debord, G. (1967/2014). *The society of the spectacle* (K. Knabb, Trans.). Bureau of Public Secrets.

Edelman, (2020). Global report. *Edelman Trust Barometer 2020*. https://www.edelman.com/sites/g/files/aatuss191/files/2020-01/2020%20Edelman%20Trust%20Barometer%20Global%20Report.pdf

Edelman, (2021). Spring update: A world in trauma. *Edelman Trust Barometer 2021*. https://www.edelman.com/sites/g/files/aatuss191/files/2021-05/2021%20Edelman%20Trust%20Barometer%20Spring%20Update_0.pdf

Fay, B. (2021, May 6). Demographics of Debt. *Demographics.org*. https://www.debt.org/faqs/americans-in-debt/demographics/

Garland, K., Wright, E., White, G., Slack, W., Rawlence, C., McLaren, I., Lambert, S., Kamlish, I., Jones, G., Higton, B., Grimbly, B., Garner, J., Froshaug, A., Fior, R., Facetti, G., Dodd, I., Crowder, H., Clift, A., ... Briggs, K. (1964). *First things first: A manifesto.*

Ghosh, S. (2021, January 17). Online misinformation about the US election fell 73% after Trump's social media ban. *Business Insider*. https://www.businessinsider.com/misinformation-fell-73-after-trump-was-banned-across-social-media-2021-1

IBM. (2020). Meet the 2020 consumers driving change [research report]. *IBM Research Insights*.

Jennings, R. (2020, February 27). Tikked off: What happens when TikTok fame fades. Vox. https://www.vox.com/the-goods/2020/2/27/21153364/tiktok-famous-backlash

Kantor, J., Weise K., and Ashford, G. (2021, June 15). Inside Amazon's employment machine. *The New York Times*. https://www.nytimes.com/interactive/2021/06/15/us/amazon-workers.html

McCarthy, Niall. (2021, June 8). Amazon warehouse injuries significantly higher than competitors. *Forbes*. https://www.forbes.com/sites/niallmccarthy/2021/06/08/amazon-warehouse-injuries-significantly-higher-than-competitors-infographic/?sh=28ee72976854

McGrath, Matt. (2021, July 1). Canada Lytton: Wildfire forces hottest place in heatwave to evacuate. *BBC News*. https://www.bbc.com/news/world-us-canada-57678054

McKenzie, L. (2021, April 27). Students want online learning options post-pandemic. *Inside Higher Ed*. https://www.insidehighered.com/news/2021/04/27/survey-reveals-positive-outlook-online-instruction-post-pandemic

Melin and Egkolfopoulou. (2021, June 1). Employees are quitting instead of giving up working from home. *Bloomberg*. https://www.bloomberg.com/news/articles/2021-06-01/return-to-office-employees-are-quitting-instead-of-giving-up-work-from-home

Morning Consult. (2019). The influencer report: Engaging gen z and millennials. https://morningconsult.com/influencer-report-engaging-gen-z-and-millennials/

Myerson, J. (2016). Scaling down: Why designers need to reverse their thinking. *She Ji Journal*, 2(4), 288–299. https://doi.org/10.1016/j.sheji.2017.06.001

Neufeld, D (2020, July 2). Visualizing the Size of Amazon, the World's Most Valuable Retailer. *Visual Capitalist*. https://www.visualcapitalist.com/amazon-worlds-most-valuable-retailer/

Papanek, V (1971). *Design for the real world: Human ecology and social change* (2 edition). Academy Chicago Publishers.

Rabin, R.C., Mandavilli, A., Hubler, S. (2021, June 29). Masks again? Delta Variant's Spread Prompts Reconsideration of Precautions. *The New York Times*. https://www.nytimes.com/2021/06/29/health/coronavirus-delta-variant-masks.html

Robbins, J. (2020, January 9). Ecopsuchology: How immersion in nature benefits your health. *Yale Environment 360*. https://e360.yale.edu/features/ecopsychology-how-immersion-in-nature-benefits-your-health

Rover, (2021, March). The pandemic pet adoption boom: What we've learned, one year later. https://www.rover.com/blog/pandemic-pet-adoption-boom/

Swanson, B. (2021, June). The anxiety of influencers: educating the tiktok generation. *Harpers*. https://harpers.org/archive/2021/06/tiktok-house-collab-house-the-anxiety-of-influencers/

Taylor, K. and Hartmans, A. (2021, March 25). Amazon drivers say peeing in bottles is 'inhumane' yet common part of the job, despite the company denying it happens. *Business Insider*. https://www.businessinsider.com/amazon-drivers-say-peeing-in-bottles-common-despite-company-denials-2021-3

Teixeira, F. (2017, June 1). Diversity by design: Our role in shaping a more inclusive industry. *R/GA by Design*. https://rgabydesign.com/diversity-by-design-our-role-in-shaping-a-more-inclusive-industry-4efccd99e1c9

Valinsky, J. (2021, May 9). Supply chain interrupted: Here's everything you can't get now. *CNN Business*. https://www.cnn.com/2021/05/08/business/supply-chain-shortages-pandemic/index.html

Vinopal, C. (2021, June 17). The pandemic forced millions out of a job. Some say they can't return to the way things were. *PBS News Hour*. /the-pandemic-forced-millions-out-of-a-job-some-say-they-cant-return-to-the-way-things-were

Wamsley, L. (2021, July 26). After tenure controversy, Nikole Hannah-Jones will join Howard faculty instead of UNC. *National Public Radio*. https://www.npr.org/2021/07/06/1013315775/after-tenure-controversy-nikole-hannah-jones-will-join-howard-faculty-instead-of

LONG PAPER

Attitudinal Design and Critique as a Wise and Responsive Deployment of Ingenuity

ANTONIA NECOCHEA PUELMA
Universidad Diego Portales
Santiago, Chile

Keywords
Speculative Design, Social Design,
Critical Design, Collaboration,
Knowledge Construction, Attitude

ABSTRACT

Design is a discipline that is being increasingly valued for its ability to address complex problems in a systematic and comprehensive way. However, Design commonly operates as a descriptive mechanism, which creates solutions to problems using mainly project-based and / or theoretical methodologies. Until now, the Design education and learning experience has been based mostly on a conventional system that generally fosters the enfolding capacities of Design, which is not negative, but does frequently promote the generation of homogeneous solutions that are often not very creative.

The following paper reviews Speculative and Critical Design as ways to promote the application of proactive mechanisms through experimental methodologies—opening up the possibility of creating new relationships and entities through the generation of questions, rather than the production of solutions to specific problems—enabling designers to position themselves on a more conscious and critical plane.

In this sense, criticism takes on an attitudinal nature, rather than being a tool or method; an attitude that allows the designer to wisely and responsively deploy ingenuity to address social, political, and cultural issues from a more conscious approach.

A BRIEF OVERVIEW OF THE ORIGINS OF DESIGN AND A BROAD IDEA OF THE CURRENT STATE OF THE DISCIPLINE

The origins of design lie in the creation of the *Staatliches Bauhaus of Weimar*, School of Design, Architecture, and Applied Arts. The Bauhaus was founded by the architect and designer Walter Gropius in Weimar, Germany in the year 1919. The school was the result of a merger between the School of Applied Arts and the School of Fine Arts "with the aim of covering all the arts of a visual and utilitarian nature in an academic space, but also a physical one, where the academicism of the liberal arts would be conjugated with the empiricism of the applied arts and there would be no class distinctions between the artist and the craftsman" (Bravo, 2015, p. 78). Here is where the normative bases and guidelines were laid down for what we know as design, establishing the academic foundations of the discipline that are still applied in design schools.

The founding of the Bauhaus took place at a time of crisis between modern thought and the rationality of technique, meaning the school was created during "a process of industrialization, in which there was a shift from artisanal production and rural societies to automated and mass production in the context of growing urbanization" (Bravo, 2015, p. 79). In this respect, the objective of the school was to reform the teaching of the arts to reclaim constructive activities and go back to doing. Walter Gropius managed the Bauhaus as director until 1928 and during that time the school was characterized by its "flexibility to adapt to political and social changes, as well as external criticism, which would be reflected in the educational and pedagogical reforms that took place over the years" (Hernández, 2004, p. 1).

After Gropius founded the school in Weimar, Germany in 1919, the Bauhaus enabled the design profession to reach new heights, "setting the foundations for its academic teaching, putting art at the service of industry, and integrating different disciplines to provide design with a character in which the real tool of work was the human mind and its perception of the image" (Bravo, 2015, p1). The most important thing for the Bauhaus, posited as the basis of the school, was the "training of being instead of doing and this is especially evident in the work of Johannes Itten, another of the founders, who proposed a *spiritual* orientation in the comprehensive training of the artist, where creativity takes precedence over technical ability" (Bravo, 2015, p. 81).

Johannes Itten, who taught at the Bauhaus between 1919 and 1923, marked the first period of the school by being the person responsible for creating a preparatory course, which guided students before they had to decide on which course, they wanted to choose for their specialization. To achieve this, he proposed a pedagogical plan that has served as a model up to the present, in which he suggested a relationship between "intuition and method or between the subjective experience and objective recognition" (Hernández, 2004, p. 1). This is how the study plan was formed for design courses, which consisted of taking the preparatory course, where the basic concepts of the discipline were taught through the investigation of the major visual components: shape, line, texture, materials, and the theory of color, before later moving on to specialized workshops; a model very similar to that currently taught in design courses at universities.

Other factors relevant to this intellectual and investigational climate were the laws of perception, otherwise known as the Gestalt laws, that were proposed by the psychologists Max Wertheimer, Wolfgang Köhler, and Kurt Koffka, who, "through various experiments, observed that the human being mentally organizes or configures forms in units or gestalts, seeking the best organization of these elements to generate a new concept based on the sum of these parts" (Bravo, 2015, p. 76).

Academically speaking, the Gestalt laws set an important precedent in the way in which schools teach design currently. Though it is not possible to state whether Gestalt determined the orientation of the inquiries about the form of the artists, or vice versa, it cannot be ruled out that there were several interpersonal contacts between Gestalt psychologists and members of the Bauhaus. Added to this, a bibliography about Gestalt laws circulated in the school and formed part of the wide theoretical corpus of those artists who tried to endow their works with conceptual basis.

The Bauhaus had three important campuses: Weimar between 1919 and 1925, Dessau between 1925 and 1932, and Berlin between 1932 and 1933. During the second half of the 20th century, the Bauhaus achieved great recognition worldwide, becoming a model for curriculum and methodological construction for many schools, to the extent that it was considered by many "not only as the first school of design academically speaking, but also as the one responsible for establishing the guidelines for these disciplines in numerous countries" (Bravo, 2015, p. 77).

As Bravo (2015) explains:

> By incorporating disciplines that ranged from visual arts to psychology, going through the hard sciences, design was given a much more formal character, in which, before a brush, or decades later, a computer, the human mind and its perception of the image would be the true tool of work (p. 75).

> The education of being above doing, applied by the Bauhaus since its beginnings, propose a spiritual orientation in the integral formation of the artist, where creativity prevails over technical ability. It is a north to consider that is applicable in the training of designers because although technical and practical knowledge are essential, creativity, and integrity will be what gives the individual the possibility to offer innovative solutions (p. 81)

As a parenthesis, it should be noted that there are many definitions of creativity, but for the purposes of this research, I will review in a broad and hasty way one of the most current ones. Robert Sternberg, American psychologist, in an interview with Saturnino de la Torre from the University of Barcelona in 2003, describes the creative person as someone who takes risks, who commits, who decides to seek new ideas, forms, and proposals; in a way, this is a person

67

who challenges the established way of doing things, transgressing what is habitual in the field of knowledge. This allows us to understand creativity as means to critique, to open discussion, generating new relationships and debate.

In 1937, László Moholy-Nagy founded the New Bauhaus in Chicago: he wished to remain faithful to the original philosophy that was grounded on the theoretical model of the unity between art and technology. However, he did introduce changes in the structure of the design curriculum, working tightly with the philosopher Charles Morris, one of the main representatives of The Vienna Circle. Morris taught a course in "intellectual integration" at the New Bauhaus in which "he attempted to articulate what he believed to be the three main dimensions of design: art, science, and technology. For various reasons, this ambitious and highly original philosophical project was never satisfactorily achieved." (Findeli, 2001, p7)

Findeli states in his article that today everybody tends to agree upon the necessity of including art, science, and technology in a design curriculum, but that disagreement will soon arise regarding the way they should be articulated. He also states that a stronger debate will arise in this matter, concerning the overall purpose of design education and practice, and asks the following questions: To which meta-project does a design project and a design curriculum contribute? For what end is design a means?

The preliminary course of the Bauhaus dictated by Johanes Itten encouraged his students to explore and to bring creativity to design. His classes began with exercises in "concentration, breathing and rhythm, the momentum of which was to flow into the student's creative work. In the process, Itten set store by subjective perception and objective understanding." (Bauhaus Kooperation, n.d.) By encouraging students to connect with their feelings and then linking that subjective approach with the objectivity of study, Itten enhanced the spirit of the school established by Gropius that encouraged each student to find their own path towards a new creation. Considering the student's experiential dimension in the design process, this not only allows them to become more intimately involved, but also gives their own tenor to both the process and the result.

On the other hand, Paul Klee, a German artist, and a *Meister* at the Bauhaus, was the one who united art with pedagogy at the school and, together with Kandinsky, Itten and Schlemmer, proposed that designing did not consist of imitating terrestrial reality, but of creating a new order. According to Klee, technique and method are the only thing that can be taught, but the *spiritual* result can only be achieved by each person on their own.

Finally, the *Hochschule fur Gestaltung* (HfG) was founded in the city of Ulm, Germany in 1950, by a group of designers led by Max Bill and Otl Aicher. Also recognized as the heir to the Bauhaus, Ulm presented a design curriculum in which the artistic dimension lost importance and the scientific content became increasingly relevant, which led to a new union: science and technology. The idea that design was applied aesthetics was replaced by a new theoretical model that considered design as an applied social and human science, where the concept of continuous experimentation and methodological research prevailed.

Like the Bauhaus from its beginnings, the Ulm school was an uncomfortable project for many people as it was considered a cosmopolitan avant-garde center, diametrically opposed to nationalism, a kind of radical rebellion against the status quo. On the other hand, the founders of this third school had considerable differences in pedagogy, and that is why in 1968 it ceased to exist. The imprint left by the school, though, was crucial to the future of design

Having outlined a brief context of the origins of design as a discipline positioned in the academic world, it seems relevant to generally review some current perspectives, to understand how the experience of education/learning in design is currently conceived.

Returning to Findeli's investigation, I would like to propose new questions, in order to broaden the subject and generate a space for reflection and discussion around design as a discipline within the academic field. Does design have a reason for being? What if design is not only a means to provide answers and solutions to complex problems, but is understood as an attitude of life capable of transforming lives?

68

Often in design schools one hears that, if the problem is well stated the solution will follow almost automatically, and though this is the most widely accepted logical structure of the design process, nothing proves that it's the only, nor the correct, one. As Moholy-Nagy used to say, "designing is a complex and intricate task. It is the integration of technological, social and economic requirements, biological necessities, and the psychophysical effects of materials, shape, color, volume, and space: thinking in relationships" (Moholy-Nagy, 1947, p. 42)

Moholy-Nagy's line of thinking leads to a new way of understanding the design process, where "instead of a problem there is a state A of a system; instead of a solution there is a state B of a system; and the designer and the user are part of the system" (Findeli, 2001, p10). The designer should be able to understand the system and develop visual intelligence that allows him/her to penetrate human needs, aspirations, fears, motivations, etc., and to understand the complexity of the outer world to, then, make new nonlinear relations.

If we accept the fact that the causal and structured problem-solution model is no longer adequate to describe every design process, due to its lack of complexity, it is pertinent to propose new curricular forms that begin to understand design as an attitude to transform life and to shift paradigms involving all aspects of one's being: intellect, imagination, sensibility, and will.

Although it has been proposed since the Bauhaus period that there should be a correspondence between method and intuition, and that subjective experience and objective recognition are directly related, it appears that this spirit has now been diluted, since it is often assumed that "knowledge is information and humans are devices to process it (...) but our knowledge consists, in the first place, of skill, and that every human being is a center of awareness and agent in the field of practice" (Ingold, 2001, p. 1). Therefore, it is not possible to attempt to dissociate the individual from their experiences and intuition. While method and theory are essential for the process, it is necessary to relate these concepts in a comprehensive manner so that the designer can be an agent of consciousness, both from and towards design.

The conceptual aspects of design are often "minimized and normalized through a reproducible 'model' of educational research that constructs a method to answer a question" (Cole & Mirzaei Rafe, 2017, p. 850). Additionally, most of these methods are project-based and/ or theoretical; that is, they generate specific solutions to specific problems, reducing the ability of design to ask questions that broaden the view of the proposed topic. In some ways, this method-centrism reduces the possibility of generating new concepts and relationships emerging directly from experimentation and reflection.

This does not mean that it is not proper to use a project-based method or that it is incorrect to aim to supply solutions to problems through design, but we must realize that each project and designer is different, so a structured model is not always the best choice. I propose to review the Bauhaus's legacy, where it is stated that creativity and production come together with the aim of imagining a new paradigm for creating art and objects, embracing all disciplines equally. It was through this convergence that Gropius managed to build a unique teaching center, in which students learned by practicing, from ceramics to typography, thus encouraging them to see the world with different eyes.

Understanding design as a discipline that involves every aspect of being, and that can challenge the established norms in order to generate new relationships, it is possible to argue that it is not only a means to find solutions to complex problems. Design becomes an attitude, critical and conscious, which is born from the designer's own process, allowing him/her to navigate the system with intuition, knowledge, and creativity.

As Cole & Mirzaei Rafe (2017) said:

> Learning therefore must be premised on collective engagement of a profound, complex, reciprocating, and rhythmic nature; since this understanding is the beginning of understanding how to map conceptual ecologies or as non-method, and nonlinear, or as fixes to educational problems, or as modes of cognitive subjectification, but as multi-level cartographies that deal with movement, change and often repeatedly entwined patternings in time/space (p. 858).

69

Finally, seeing design as an attitude allows the designer to work with rhythmic processes, their own methods, and in a non-linear way. If the *design problem* is understood as a multilevel system that is in constant motion, there will be greater flexibility to approach its complexity with awareness and criticism.

By generating a space for criticism, it is possible to reflect, question the established norms, and generate new relationships, and if this exercise is carried out in a collaborative and interdisciplinary way, then it could be said that design goes to another level. Understanding design as an attitude allows the discipline to be placed on a plane in which not only complex problems are solved, but also social, political, and environmental issues can be approached proactively, moving towards the creation of innovative futures.

CASE STUDY: A BRIEF OVERVIEW OF THE HISTORY, AND A BROAD IDEA OF THE CURRENT STATE, OF DESIGN EDUCATION IN CHILE

Before the existence of design courses in Chile, formal teaching of Fine Arts was introduced with the opening of the Painting Academy in 1849 directed by Alejandro Cicarelli due to a concern of the government for the promotion of fine arts. It should be noted that the first generation of artists in Chile was trained during this foundational stage of artistic education, and they subsequently worked as calligraphers, caricaturists, engravers, illustrators, lithographers, and typographers, later becoming an important part of the first design schools at universities in two of the main cities of the country, Valparaiso in 1967 and Santiago in 1969.

As said above, the Bauhaus was created in Weimar between the two world wars in 1919 and, at the same time, there was the explosion of the so-called *typographic revolution* that came along with the Industrial Revolution. These events led Moholy-Nagy to introduce typography as a preliminary course in the Bauhaus in 1923, demanding absolute clarity in every typographic work in order to establish a new typographic language that combined elasticity, variety and a fresh use of the print materials. These two events were an important milestone in design education around the world, and would have local repercussions years later. During the 1910s and 1920s, various artistic avant-garde groups began developing that preceded the formation of Graphic Design as an independent profession of the Fine Arts. Although the methodological approach of the Bauhaus was not very widely received in Chile during its boom period, it did have certain influence in one sector of education years afterwards.

In 1928, by decree of the then-Minister of Public Education, Pablo Ramírez, the Academy of Fine Arts was arbitrarily closed. Ramírez tried to compensate for this by sending a group of 30 artists to continue training in Europe, so they returned to Chile with the mission of "breaking the old preconceptions of the Academy of Fine Arts and assimilating new techniques and knowledge in the old continent" (Álvarez Caselli, 2004, p. 100). Around 1929 a project was started with the aim of training people who were capable of putting the visual arts at the service of industry. The reform of the statutes of the School of Fine Arts under the management of Carlos Isamitt "resulted in the separation of the decorative art section and the subsequent creation of the School of Applied Arts, which was completely autonomous and had its premises, but forming part of the Universidad de Chile" (Álvarez Caselli, 2004, p. 101)

In 1953, former Bauhaus academic Josef Albers, who had taught the *Vorkurs* at the Bauhaus and who in those years directed the Department of Design at Yale University, came to the School of Architecture of the *Pontificia Universidad Católica de Chile* and worked with Alberto Piwonka, architect of the same university, to teach the Preliminary Bauhaus Course in Chile. As Álvarez Caselli states in his book, this course, historically linked to the debate on modernization and the connections between artistic and project disciplines, had a particular insertion in Chile. As this course transitioned from pedagogical reformism and abstract art to visual perception and color studies, the long journey of this course at the Faculty of Architecture and Fine Arts of *Pontificia Universidad Católica de Chile* allow us to crosswise reconstruct the history of pedagogical modernization in Chile within the disciplines of architecture, art, and design.

70

Although the creation of design schools was a great advance for the discipline, Álvarez Caselli explains that there was some growing disinterest from those who had been self-taught in the graphic area in Chile during the first half of the 20th century, mainly because there was a generalized idea that it was not possible to study design at an institution, rather that the designer had to be trained during practice.

Design schools appeared in Chile after the university reform in 1967; a reform that brought structural changes, allowing the economic incorporation of a broader spectrum of society that revealed other difficulties and inequalities. Superior education in Chile transits from a long republican foundational time since 1842, to profound change and reform between 1960 and 1970. "This reform period took place in a context of political change that impacted the universities in their governance models, laid the foundations for research, increased public resources and expanded enrollment to much higher levels than the previous period." (Menéndez, 2014, p.135).

In the sixties, there were eight universities in Chile, *Universidad de Chile* was the one with most presence with its schools in Santiago and Valparaíso. Almost at the end of the decade, the mobilizations for university reform sought not only changes in the treatment of higher education from the Government, the State, and the Ministry of Education, but also relevant changes in the ways universities were conceived by their own communities.

Educational conflict extended mainly between 1967 and 1973—1967 and 1968 being the years of greatest intensity—and education was suspended along with the interruption of democracy on September 11, 1973. The reform caused universities to be politicized, and at the same time the important organizational and academic transformation was kept silent, which implied a great effort to promote scientific, technological, and cultural development within the universities.

After the reform, the first programs based on the *Vorkurs* or Preliminary Course at the Bauhaus were developed. "The embryonic training-professional stage conducted by the traditional universities had a technical-intuitive beginning, aimed at solving problems that promoted quality of life and technological development" (Álvarez Caselli, 2004, p. 133).

According to Alain Findeli (2001) in his article *Rethinking Design Education for the 21st Century*, the discipline has adopted two major paradigms to account for the logics of design thinking: applied art and applied science. At present, the methodological approach that is most often used globally to conduct the design process is project-based, positioning the discipline as an applied science, meaning that:

1. A need, or problem, is identified: situation **A**;

2. A final goal, or solution, is imagined and described: situation **B**; and

3. The act of design is the causal link by which situation **A** is transformed into situation **B**

As such, the concept of project gains a much stronger theoretical status. Instead of "applied" science, I propose to speak of "involved," "situated," or "embedded" science. Such a model considers that the scientific inquiry and attitude are carried into (instead of applied to) the field of the project and of practice so that the former are modified by the latter, and vice versa. (p. 10)

Although certain modifications have been made in the design curriculum and programs over time, the essence of the Chilean design schools that appeared after the reform has been maintained, preserving an approach that prioritizes the technical nature of the discipline over the exchange of artistic experiences, which has meant that the interest in exploring non-traditional forms of expression has been gradually diluted.

In most design schools in Chile, if not all, designers work with certain methodologies established as the *correct ones*, based mainly on setting up a problem and finding a solution for that problem. An example of this is that every time one looks to do something related to innovation, the Design Thinking method developed by IDEO is used, perhaps excessively. Some design programs use this method, almost exclusively, to approach the design process, generating homogenous projects with less purposeful results.

This does not mean that it is wrong to use methodologies such as Design Thinking, on the contrary, it is a great approach for certain projects. But it is necessary to understand that design is

71

not always linear and that many times it is not just about finding answers, but about raising new questions that allow us to broaden the subject, in order to have a general view of the system. Being able to understand the multilevel nature of the theme, question what has been established and explore different possibilities, allows openings to new types of solutions.

According to various authors, the world is going through a period of constant change, so, responding to the rapid transformations that have occurred in recent years, it is essential to rethink the education and practice of design with a view to a constantly changing future. It is because of this, and because each project has a different nature, that it seems proper to promote the incorporation of a broader vision of design in academic curricula. Encouraging students to adopt design as an attitude allows them to work collaboratively, with their own processes and based on exploration. Releasing their security, so that they dare to question the obvious, makes them more conscious and purposeful designers.

SPECULATIVE DESIGN AS THE DRIVING FORCE BEHIND THE DESIGN PROCESS

Speculative Design was inspired by the Critical Architecture of the 1960s. Anthony Dunne and Fiona Raby were among the first to use the term in the 1970s, and have since explored how "this spirit could be reintroduced to contemporary design and how design's boundaries could be extended beyond the strictly commercial to embrace the extreme, the imaginative, and the inspiring" (Dunne & Raby, 2013, p. 6).

One of the main reasons design is valued is because of its capacity to address complex problems in a systematic and comprehensive manner. However, there are infinite possibilities in the discipline that go beyond linear problem-solving—one of them proposes design as a means of speculating about how things could be, through the creation of multiple paths and perspectives to address a certain problem or proposition.

As Dunne and Raby (2013) explain:

> This form of design thrives on imagination and aims to open new perspectives on what are sometimes called wicked problems, to create spaces for discussion and debate about alternative ways of being, and to inspire and encourage people's imaginations to flow freely. Design speculations can act as a catalyst for collectively redefining our relationship to reality (p. 2).

The starting point of speculative design work is usually asking, *what would happen if?* This creates a space for debate and criticism, giving the design process a provocative and fictitious nature that "requires viewers to suspend their disbelief and allow their imaginations to wander, to momentarily forget how things are now, and wonder about how things could be" (Dunne & Raby, 2013, p. 3). In order to achieve this, Dunne and Raby propose that we should look beyond

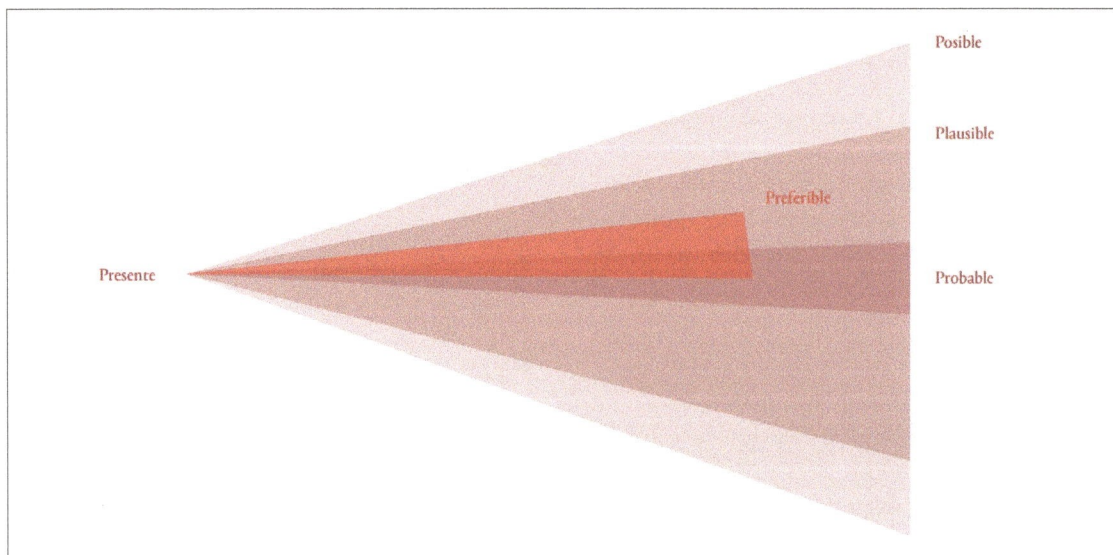

Figure 1: PPPP diagram, Dunne & Raby, 2013, p. 5; reformatted by author.

design, towards the methodological fields of other disciplines such as literature, film, politics, and art; "to explore, hybridize, borrow, and embrace the many tools available for crafting not only things but also ideas" (Dunne & Raby, 2013, p. 3).

In their book *Speculative Everything*, one of the best-known publications in the field of Speculative Design, Dunne and Raby explain how design can operate in different possible imaginaries by creating four future scenarios: *Probable Future, Plausible Future, Possible Future, and Preferable Future* (see Figure 1). Each of these scenarios is briefly explained below for contextualization:

Probable Future: this is described as what is likely to happen, unless there is a specific event that produces something different. Most designers currently operate in this plane, since "most design methods, processes, tools, acknowledged good practice, and even design education are oriented toward this space" (Dunne & Raby, 2013, p. 3).

Plausible Future: this is a place of scenario planning and foresight, which suggests there is a space for what could happen if all the optimal conditions are in place for it to occur. By exploring alternative economic and political futures, various ways are suggested in which an organization will be prepared for and thrive in various futures.

Possible Future: this is a scenario in which links are made between today's world and the suggested one, where "a believable series of events that led to the new situation is necessary, even if entirely fictional. This allows viewers to relate the scenario to their own world and to use it as an aid for critical reflection. This is the space of speculative culture" (Dunne & Raby, 2013, p. 4).

Preferable Future: this is the space of intersection between the Probable Future and Plausible Future, but which leads to the question of who decides what is preferable for people, companies, and the government? This leads to the suggestion that design should operate in a Possible Future, as a means to open up all sorts of possibilities that can be discussed, debated, and used to "collectively define a preferable future for a given group of people .... design can give experts permission to let their imaginations flow freely, give material expression to the insights generated

... and provide platforms for further collaborative speculation" (Dunne & Raby, 2013, p. 6).

After examining the four scenarios in which design can operate, it seems consistent to suggest that design as a discipline could use Speculative Design as one of the driving forces behind the process, in order to explore new forms and create new relationships. On the other hand, considering the transformations through which the world is currently going, and understanding that the new generations have different motivations than those that came before them, it is essential to understand that "now, a younger generation doesn't dream, it hopes; it hopes that we will survive, that there will be water for all, that we will be able to feed everyone, that we will not destroy ourselves.... there has been a new wave of interest in thinking about alternatives to the current system" (Dunne & Raby, 2013, p. 9), and this supports the idea that it is necessary to generate instances that provide a space to propose new options for the world in the not-too-distant future. Once it is accepted that design is more than the aesthetics and functionality of products, and that it has a value that transcends designer self-promotion and the idea that communication is in the service of industry, it is possible to understand it as a discipline that is "socially engaged for raising awareness; satire and critique; inspiration, reflection, highbrow entertainment; aesthetic explorations; speculation about possible futures; and as a catalyst for change" (Dunne & Raby, 2013, p. 33).

CRITICAL DESIGN AS AN ATTITUDE

Critical Design is a term coined by Dunne and Raby in the mid-1990s, and it emerged from the need to propose a way to politely refute what already exists, in order to open the space to dream, wish, and even entertain illusions. The authors propose criticism as an attitude, rather than a movement, which is not necessarily negative, but demonstrates a contrasting position to positivist design, understanding that there can be a diversity of possible methodologies, views, and approaches to address the same issue. "Critical Design uses Speculative Design proposals to challenge narrow assumptions, preconceptions, and givens" (Dunne & Raby, 2013, p. 34). Suggesting how things could be and proposing alternatives to what already exists can promote the awareness of existing weaknesses

73

or shortcomings in what is currently considered normal; so, the generation of critical thinking assumes that things are not taken for granted, but rather that the designer is skeptical and questions things as they are known at present.

Questioning what exists and not taking anything for granted opens the way for exploration, enabling the designer to experiment by assuming different roles and becoming aware of various problems, rather than just one in particular. Various discourses are constructed through Critical Design from which unresolved tensions are evidenced regarding the issues in question that it does not intend to solve, but rather to expose for reflection and debate in a collaborative way. If this approach is understood as a form of design thinking that is present during the design process, greater commitment from the designer can be generated through the establishment of open discourse that allows the creation of a reflective environment, giving space to create their own way of thinking and reflecting through experimentation. The aim of criticism is to make people aware, "to provoke a change of opinion, deepen the meaning of things, and not just remaining with what is exposed in its most superficial form ... arguing in favor of criticism as an agent of change that is capable of transforming" (Fern, 2015, p. 32).

It is currently argued that design is mainly aimed at solving problems, as a mechanism that provides answers to the problems posed, essentially through the use of project-based methodologies founded on theory and research. In this regard, design is proposed as a complete process, capable of providing the designer with the necessary tools to solve complex problems systematically.

A Critical Design attitude is perceived as a more radical position of design, which is proposed as a comprehensive reflective process, giving rise to questions about questions, through constant exploration at all times and throughout the process. This creates an environment that is conducive to creating new relationships and promoting debate, which enables citizens to be positioned as people, rather than users or consumers, and understanding the issues raised as areas of exploration, instead of problems to be solved.

A great example of Speculative Critical Design (SCD) is the Microbial Home by Philips Design Probe Program, that was presented for the Dutch Design Week in 2011, in Eindhoven, Germany. This home is a domestic ecosystem challenging conventional design solutions to energy, cleaning, food preservation, lighting, waste and the idea of a healthy lifestyle in general. It states that humans have been part of the biological fragility placed upon the earth, playing an important role in the collapse of its delicate balance.

In this probe, Philips ask questions about the viability of biological processes in our homes and places of work, being critical about the resources we have in our homes, the amount of waste we generate and the way to manage it. The Microbial Home critiques how the demands generated from the systems and utilities of modern lifestyles are disconnected, wasteful and inefficient. Perhaps there is no single way to solve the problem, perhaps there is no solution, and the impact can only be lessened. Philips asks the following question, "What if there is a way of thinking about energy, sanitation, water, cooling, light and heating, not as discrete systems but parts of a natural system that minimizes the waste we produce?"

To fully understand the impact that SCD has when one adopts it as an attitude, it's worth checking out an article written by Rose Etherington in *Dezeen Magazine*, where she explains the following:

> Probes projects are intended to understand future sociocultural and technological shifts with a view to developing nearer-term scenarios. These scenario explorations are often carried out in collaboration with experts and thought leaders in different fields, culminating in a 'provocation' designed to spark discussion and debate around new ideas and lifestyle concepts.

> The Design Probe projects carried out by Philips Design are part of a wider Philips strategy aimed at improving the innovation hit rate. While it is not intended that design concepts coming out of the Probes program are translated to marketable solutions, insights gained from debate around the concepts feed into future innovation for the company.

74

Philips Design's creative force of some 400 professionals, representing more than 35 different nationalities, embraces disciplines as diverse as psychology, cultural sociology, anthropology, and trend research in addition to the more 'conventional' design-related skills. (Etherington, 2011)

This gives rise to the creation of discursive design, in which "the creation of objects and services goes beyond their utilitarian function, but is rather perceived as a diffuser of ideas, provoking debate, awareness, and generation of knowledge" (Fern, 2015, p. 43). SCD is means by which one can speculate by presenting questions that allow reflection and exploration of ethical, social, and political issues in the context of daily life. If design is conceived from its critical capacity, it is possible to generate a "debate about various topics through exploration, enabling explanation, questioning, provoking action, dissemination, raising awareness, and offering new perspectives" (Fern, 2015, p. 61).

In the way in which design is currently perceived, we can observe a strong inclination towards the excessive use of methodologies. This method-centrism encourages the use of descriptive and project-based mechanisms to provide solutions to problems systematically, leading to the creation of linear solutions, because of the lack of a space that enables the designer to be free and autonomous to reflect and make new relationships.

With this paper, I propose to question the design process and the experience of education/learning of the discipline, to review the possibility of incorporating Speculative Critical Design as an attitude, especially when it is necessary to explore new scenarios. Applying SCD to broaden discussion, mainly in projects in which the design process is used as a method of research and intellectual study, or in initiatives that are linked to ecological and/or social design, promotes the capacities of the discipline to generate new relationships, often in a collaborative and interdisciplinary way. When one speculates and thinks of future scenarios, the possibility of exploration and experimentation opens, allowing them to take place in unforeseen instances of conversation and reflection.

Alice Rawsthorne (2019) states the following, regarding her book *Design as an Attitude*:

László Moholy-Nagy's ambitious and eclectic vision of designers as free made him realize that clichés have to be crushed and the only way to do that is for Design, whether attitudinal, professional, or otherwise, to prove its worth in new terrain. Why else would politicians, bureaucrats, NGOs, and investors think that design is capable of redesigning health systems or developing them more efficiently? ... Design can only play a more prominent and powerful role in our lives if it demonstrates that it deserves it. With greater responsibilities and scale of ambition it could be very difficult to achieve this, but it is absolutely necessary, otherwise Design will not earn the public and political support it needs to continue.

Having established a brief context about the origins of design and the way in which the discipline is currently perceived, it can be seen that the technical nature of design is often prioritized, which has gradually diluted the interest in exploring non-formal, non-traditional forms. The design process must be understood as an instance for the designer to build his/her discourse based on exploration, intuition and objective understanding. Understanding and projecting design as an attitude allows promoting the capacities of autonomy, collaboration, and reflection through the appropriation of themes through speculation and transformation of what already exists.

For all the reasons mentioned above, it seems pertinent to open a debate on the process of design education/learning. The trend towards the academization of experience, through the transfer of information in a manner that is often unilateral in a classroom that appears to be a rigid and inflexible space, has led to an attempt to rationalize the education of the discipline by adapting it to closed concepts. The use of specific teaching methods to formulate and disseminate design methodologies and the characterization of problems means that, in many cases, designers incorporate the use of descriptive and project-based mechanisms from the start, in order to provide solutions to problems systematically, without leaving room for exploration and experimentation of new scenarios and ways of approaching both the design process and what results from it.

75

If critical speculative thinking is applied to understand how this way of conceiving design could be used in the classroom, it would be interesting to ask questions that allow us to open up each topic, instead of simply providing a single answer. What if the work is not about solving a specific problem? What if the student is asked to speculate on a social and/or environmental issue, in order to imagine a possible future? What if one worked with methodologies from other disciplines, or collaborative work was done with other careers?

REFERENCES

Augé, M. (1992). *Los "no lugares" espacios del anonimato. Una Antropología De La Sobremodernidad.* (1ra. ed., pp. 1-67). Barcelona, Spain: Gedisa Editorial

Bateson, G. (1987). *Steps To an ecology of mind.* (2da. ed., pp. 1-353). United States: Jason Aronson Inc.

Bravo, R. (2015). Vigencia de la Bauhaus en la formación académica de los Diseñadores Gráficos. *Calle 14: Revista de investigación en el campo del arte,* 10(15), pp. 72-82. Retrieved from https://www.redalyc.org/articulo.oa?id=279044557008

Cambariere, L. (2005). Una charla de diseño: Gui Bonsiepe. *Página 12,* pp. 10-15. Retrieved from http://www.guibonsiepe.com/pdffiles/entrevista_pagina12.pdf

Cole, D. & Mirzaei Rafe, M. (2017). Conceptual ecologies for educational research through Deleuze, Guattari and Whitehead. *International Journal of Qualitative Studies in Education,* 30(9), pp. 849-862. Retrieved from https://www.researchgate.net/publication/318240741_Conceptual_ecologies_for_educational_research_through_Deleuze_Guattari_and_Whitehead

Design Council. (2017). Design for change, (n/a), pp. 1-16. Retrieved from https://www.designcouncil.org.uk/what-we-do/design-training-and-education/design-academy

Domínguez, F. & Fogué, U. (2017). Desplegando las capacidades políticas del diseño. *Revista Diseña Escuela de Diseño Pontificia Universidad Católica de Chile,* 11, p. 96-109. Retrieved from http://www.revistadisena.com/desplegando-las-capacidades-politicas-del-diseno/

Dunne, A. & Raby, F. (2013). *Speculative Everything.* (1st ed., pp. 1-236). London, England: MIT Press

Etherington, R. (29 October 2011). *Microbial Home by Philips Design.* Retrieved from https://www.dezeen.com/2011/10/29/microbial-home-by-philips-design/

Fern, I. (2015). (Unpublished doctoral thesis). Universidad Autónoma de Barcelona, Barcelona, Spain.

Ferruzca, M. (2015). Aproximaciones conceptuales para entender el diseño en el siglo XXI, (n/a), pp. 1-280. Retrieved from https://www.researchgate.net/publication/282136684

Findeli, A. (2001). Rethinking Design Education for the 21st Century: Theoretical, Methodological, and Ethical Discussion. *MIT Press Journals* (Eds.), 17(1), pp. 5-17. Retrieved from https://www.mitpressjournals.org/doi/pdf/10.1162/07479360152103796

Flores, F. (1992), *La Era del Cambio,* (video file). Retrieved from https://www.youtube.com/watch?v=WEnSPZhtoyE

Hernández, B. (2004). Bauhaus, la escuela que unió arte y técnica. *Técnica Industrial,* 252, pp. 68-74. Retrieved from http://www.tecnicaindustrial.es/TIFrontal/a-1676-bauhaus-escuela-unio-arte-tecnica.aspx

Ingold, T. (2001). From the transmission of representations to the education of attention. The Debated Mind: Evolutionary psychology versus ethnography (n/a, pp. 113-153). Berg, Oxford: H. Whitehouse.

Kerridge, T. (2016). Designing Debate: The Entanglement of Speculative Design and Upstream Engagement. *Design Research Society,* (n/a), pp. 1-12. Retrieved from https://research.gold.ac.uk/18818/1/Kerridge-designingdebate.pdf

Malpass, M. (2015). Criticism and Function in Critical Design Practice. *MIT Press Journals* (Eds.), 31(2), pp. 59-71. Retrieved from https://www.mitpressjournals.org/doi/pdf/10.1162/DESI_a_00322

Max Neef, M. (1998). *Desarrollo a escala humana.* (2da. ed., pp. 1-150). Barcelona, Spain: Nordan e Icaria

Moholy-Nagy, L. (1947). Vision in Motion, Chicago, USA.

Navarro, F., Vinicio, M., Fulco Rinaldi, D., Jiménez, A., Gazano, J. I., & Revueltas, J. (2015), *Aproximaciones conceptuales para entender el diseño en el siglo XXI,* (n/a), pp. 1-280. Retrieved from https://www.researchgate.net/publication/282136684_Aproximaciones_para_entender_el_diseno_en_el_siglo_XXI

Palmerino, D. (2004). La Bauhaus y el Diseño [Thesis Project not published]. Universidad Abierta Interamericana

Pino, B., Conti, G., & Galli, F. (2013). Towards a Cross Cultural Society; from ethnicity to design, "narrative" heritage drives innovation. *Cumulus DUOC 2012,* (n/a), pp. 173-177. Retrieved from https://www.researchgate.net/publication/274381468_Towards_a_Cross_Cultural_Society_from_ethnicity_to_design_narrative_heritage_drives_innovation

Piscitelli, A. (2014). *Introducción al diseño especulativo: ficción, hackeo y social dreaming.* Retrieved from http://catedradatos.com.ar/2014/06/introduccion-al-diseno-especulativo/

Rawsthorne, A. [theaspeninstitute. (June 26, 2019). Design as an Attitude [video file]. Retrieved from https://www.youtube.com/watch?v=7Tlsi5BsaL0

Schensul, J. & LeCompte, M. (2013). *Essential Etnographic Methods.* (2nd ed., pp. 1-387). Plymouth, United Kingdom: Altamira Press

Thackara, J. (2005). *In the bubble: designing in a complex world.* (n/a, pp. 211-226, London, England: MIT Press

Tironi, M. (2017). Repensando la política desde el Diseño (y el Diseño desde la política). *Revista Diseña,* 11, pp. 3-45. Retrieved from http://www.revistadisena.com/repensando-la-politica-desde-el-diseno-y-el-diseno-desde-la-politica/

Triggs, T. (2011). Graphic design history: Past, present, and future. *MIT Press Journals* (Eds.), 27, pp. 3-6. Retrieved from https://www.mitpressjournals.org/doi/pdf/10.1162/desi_a_00051

Torre, S. D. L, Barrios, O & Tejada Fernandez, J. (2000). *Estrategias didácticas innovadoras. Recursos para la formación y el cambio.* (1 ed.) (Recursos, 31).

Designing Situated Learning Environments for Media Design Education: A Case Study

SARAH LUGTHART AND MICHEL VAN DARTEL
Centre of Applied Research for
Art, Design and Technology, Avans
University of Applied Sciences
Netherlands

Keywords
Situated learning, Media design
education, Authentic learning,
Learning environments

INTRODUCTION

Higher vocational design education aims to prepare students for careers as design professionals. Besides providing design skills and theory, such education generally also involves the provision of situated learning experiences. Such are experiences in which learning occurs through the social interaction and kinesthetic activity of real-life activities in the context of a prospective practice or related tasks (Northern Illinois University Center for Innovative Teaching and Learning, 2012). "Just as a designer is expected to work 'in the wild', it is reasonable to think that the education itself should take place in the complex use-contexts students are expected to design for" (Wärnestål & Lindqvist, 2013, p.181). Although situated learning experiences are traditionally organized through placements outside of the school environment, more recently, innovative models to introduce students to complex use-contexts within the school environment have gained popularity (Herrington, 2015; Roach et al., 2018). In such innovative models the cognitive realism of the learning experiences (e.g., the authenticity of the decision-making processes) is generally deemed more important for learners than its physical realism (i.e., the authenticity of their physical setting).

Media design is an evolving field in which graphic arts meets digital technology and that "involves the physical, functional, and operational manifestation of human-factors design" (Garson & Khosrowpour, 2007, p. 661). It includes subdomains varying from animation and games to VFX and motion design. As media design is particular in that it "requires an understanding of the multisensory nature of the user's experience and applying human learning, memory, messaging, perception, and cognition" (ibid., p. 661), vocational media design education could arguably benefit even more from situated learning experiences than traditional design paradigms can. Although ample research has been conducted on designing situated learning environments for specific educational models (e.g., constructivism (Kafai, 2006), connectivism (Griffiths & Guile, 2003) and problem-based learning (Barrett, 2010)), for education in general (see, e.g., Choi & Hannafin, 1995; Herrington & Oliver, 2000 or Shaltry et al., 2013), and for design education (see, e.g., Simonsen et al., 2014), the design of situated learning environments for media design education deserves specific attention given its potential merit for such education. Therefore, we formulated the following research question:

How should situated learning environments be designed for media design education?

To answer this research question, we conducted a case study. In this study we observed the behavior of students working on assignments by real-life clients, in media design studios that were simulated within their school environment. In this paper, we will first discuss the principles of situated learning in relation to media design education. We will then present our case study in more detail and present our case study results, after which we will discuss these results and draw conclusions.

77

SITUATED LEARNING IN MEDIA DESIGN EDUCATION

Donaldson & Barany (2019) distinguish three core features of situated learning: communities of practice, participation, and authentic context. The first core feature of situated learning, communities of practice, refers to the sociocultural specificity of a community of practitioners: the term is used to conceptualize groups that form around shared patterns of behavior. According to Lave & Wenger (1991), the most important aspect of a situated learning experience is that they provide learners access to a "community of practice". In media design education, shared patterns of behavior can, for instance, be observed in how media designers typically pitch concepts to clients. Such behavior is socioculturally determined by the community, even though specific details can differ substantially between media design studios. Hence, a community of practice does not only consist of a collection of "hard skills" (i.e., technical skills) typical for a domain; shared patterns of behavior also form around "soft skills" (i.e., the interpersonal skills required to perform a role) typical for its practitioners.

The second core feature of situated learning, participation, refers to if and how students get to explore which roles or activities inside a community of practice fit their talents and skills, as well as their preferred way of working. Such exploration is crucial for learners to "try on" different roles and identities (Donaldson & Barany, 2019). Scaffolding can be required to facilitate a learner in growing from newcomer to full participant (Donaldson & Barany, 2019).

The third core feature of situated learning is authentic context, meaning "robust, complex, social environments made up of actors, actions, and situations" (Stein, 1998, p. 2). To bridge the gap between the school environment and real-life practices "the learning context and the activities within that context are meaningful [in providing] the opportunities necessary to solve problems practically so [students] can transfer those competencies to real-world experiences" (DiSchiavi, 2019). When such learning environments are cooperative in nature, they enhance social interaction and enable learners to challenge each other (NIU-CITL, 2012). This collaborative aspect also adds to the complexity and authenticity of the (learning) environment.

CASE STUDY: PROJECT SOHO

During every first half of the second semester, the Master Animation of the Master Institute of Visual Cultures (MIVC, The Netherlands) simulates small studios modeled after the media design studios situated in close proximity to each other in Soho, the bustling creative heart of London. *Project Soho*, as the temporary studios are collectively named, aims to familiarize students with the hard and soft skills that an animation studio requires. The working period in one of *Project Soho*'s temporary studios allows students to discover what their preferred role in the creative practice of animation might be. In 2020, twenty-two international students participated in *Project Soho* for eight weeks from February until April. Each year, the simulation is split up in three phases: 1) set up, 2) working, 3) self-evaluation.

Set up

In preparation for *Project Soho*, tutors group students in productive mixes of competencies and skills based on their backgrounds and individual learning goals. Each group (studio) subsequently appoints a producer as well as a main contact for future clients. Each group is also required to set up a "studio agreement", that includes the studio's name, mission statement, division of tasks, and summarizes organizational matters such as the frequency of meetings and software used to communicate and organize their work. After explaining the intentions of *Project Soho* and what is expected from students during the working period, tutors distribute a diversity of assignments for animation studios among the groups. These assignments are requested from real-life clients connected to the MIVC network. For the purpose of our case study, in the set-up phase, we collected copies of all studio agreements and recorded our (natural) observations of students on the basis of written event sampling (Lewis-Beck, Bryman, & Futing Liao, 2004).

Working

In the working phase, assignments from clients — ranging from assignments for tv-commercials, to interactive book trailers, to music videos — are distributed at irregular frequencies via email. Without knowing if or when another assignment might come in, a studio chooses to accept or

78

decline each assignment. Studios can also agree to work together on an assignment. After accepting an assignment, the studio meets with the client to discuss the design brief. Afterwards, clients remain available for feedback, to receive pitches of ideas, and to respond to any issue or question that may arise during the design process. Tutors have weekly meetings with each studio to monitor and discuss their progress on the assignments. This happens on the basis of a log, in which each studio reports issues that the group encountered and reflects on their progress and process. Students meet and work on the assignments at school or from home. In the middle of the working period, studio members are requested to use the 360-degrees feedback method (Kaya, Aydin & Durgut, 2016) to provide each other with feedback on performance within the studio. After an assignment is completed, clients organize a debrief with the studio in which clients provide feedback on how well the product matches their expectations, as well as on how professionally the students worked and communicated. For the purpose of our case study, copies of the logs of each studio were collected as well as copies of their 360-degrees feedback forms.

Evaluation

Finally, after completing all assignments that the studio accepted and presenting all their products to their clients, individual members of each studio hand in a self-reflection form that invites them to reflect on the various roles they performed in the studio and evaluate their overall learning experience. For the purpose of our case study, copies of these self-reflection forms were collected.

RESULTS

Our case study yielded nine insights, during the set-up (3), working (4), and evaluation (2) phase, that are relevant to our research question, *How should situated learning environments be designed for media design education?*

Set-up phase results

The *set-up* phase of our case study yielded copies of the agreements of five studios: *Anima Mea, Cosmosfox, Monstera, Magic Lantern*, and *Red Duke*. Our observations in this phase were done during a field trip to a media design studio and during the deliberation of students about their

studio agreements. During the field trip, students were acquainted with examples of the roles and responsibilities within a media design studio (e.g., storyboard artist, lead animator, technical director, (creative) director and producer). After the field trip, students met to discuss the division of roles within their own studios. We gained three important insights from these deliberations among students (studio members) during this first step in setting up a studio agreement.

First, we gained the insight that taking up the role of producer was always met with some hesitation. Two out of five groups even decided to divide this task between two members. Secondly, we gained the insight that students struggled to estimate the amount of work that comes with a certain role or responsibility. Frequently raised questions are, for instance, related to how many assignments could be completed within the working period and how many different responsibilities one can take up at one time. A third insight from observing the deliberations among studio members is that most studios agreed to assign roles to individual members for the whole working period. Only one of the five studio agreements (by *Red Duke*) included the rule that each studio member could try various roles throughout the working period.

Working phase results

The *working* phase yielded copies of the complete logs of each of the five studios, as well as 22 self-reflection forms. These logs and forms gave rise to four additional insights, related to the 1) quality of feedback, 2) quality of self-reflection, 3) need for scaffolding, and 4) validation of roles.

The insight regarding *quality of feedback* relates to the finding that three logs (of the five logs collected in total) referred to a discomfort experienced by studio members in providing their fellow members with critical feedback. In the *Monstera* log, for instance, a member states that: "One of my biggest concerns was to offend someone with my feedback. Especially, at the beginning I tried to be very careful with it. Later, I began to notice that our team work improved when we were more honest to each other." Furthermore, the logs show that the quality of feedback is related to how transparent clients are about their expectations. For example, the log of *Anima Mea* stated that a client had temporarily

79

stepped out of its role to allow for elaboration on industry expectations regarding the quality of pitches in response to a pitch document that the studio presented. Had this situation occurred in real life, the client would most likely not have taken the time to explain to the studio in detail why their pitch did not convince. In a simulation like *Project Soho*, clients are aware of the educational value of good feedback and, as the log of *Anima Mea* demonstrates, may temporarily step out of their role of client to increase the quality of their feedback. This makes the insight we gained regarding the quality of feedback in situated learning experiences two-fold: it depends on transparency between studio members, yet also on whether or not clients are willing, allowed, and able to temporarily step into the role of educator.

The insight we gained regarding the *quality of self-reflection* is based on the fact that some logs described every single task conducted by each member, while other studios simply copy-pasted written feedback from a client into their log and merely added some notes on their response to it. This provided us with the insight that the ways in which logs are used within a studio range from keeping detailed descriptions of all steps taken in the processes to reporting on progress in a more general and reflective way.

The insight regarding the *need for scaffolding* is based on the fact that three logs explicitly expressed a need for more tutoring, while self-evaluation forms reported conflicting needs: for some, the absence of tutors was beneficial to the learning experience; others missed the support. One member of studio *Cosmosfox*, for instance, stated in its self-evaluation that "Having more guest lectures of people who work with clients would have helped ease some anxiety and doubt about our roles", while the self-evaluation form of another *Cosmosfox* studio member included the statement that participating in budget break-downs, debriefings and contact with clients in the absence of tutors provided "insight in the practice, and also made [the studio member] feel more comfortable in [their] position." This provided us with the insight that the *need for scaffolding* can differ between individual students and that these individual needs can even be conflicting.

The insight regarding the *validation of roles* stems from the data collected during the working phase,

which shows that roles within studios were fluid: all five logs contained statements referring to members helping each other to complete projects, particularly near the end of the working period. The *Cosmosfox* studio log also reveals a reason behind their willingness to do work beyond their individual roles and responsibilities: "We care more about functioning as one strong team, then about individual projects." This provided us with the insight that trying out different roles during the simulation has value beyond the room to explore how well various roles fit a studio member: it can also enhance the group dynamic within a team.

Evaluation phase results

The *evaluation phase* of our case study yielded twenty-two self-reflection forms completed by students at the end of the working period. These forms gave rise to two insights, regarding 1) the professional behavior within the community of practice, and 2) the exploration of different roles and identities.

The first insight is that students learned what professional *behavior within a community of practice* entails from their participation in the simulation. This can be illustrated with a quote from the self-evaluation form of a member of *Anima Mea*: "I realize now that working on Saturdays and Sundays [...] not only has a mental and physical impact, but can also have a financial impact. My time is worth money." Additionally, at least eight forms refer to the importance of good communication. A member of *Monstera* mentions that "[the] biggest lesson I learned is the importance of good communication within the team; it can literally make or break projects."

Finally, the second insight is that students learned from *the exploration of different roles* and identities within their design studio. This insight is based on the many statements in the self-reflection forms that allude to a growth in confidence with respect to fulfilling certain roles and identities after experiencing them first-hand. For example, a studio member of *Red Duke* stated: "I feel more confident now to present myself as an all-around 3D artist when applying for jobs."

In the next section, we will discuss these results from our case study on the basis of the three core features of situated learning.

DISCUSSION

Our case study resulted in nine insights that are relevant to answer our research question: *how should situated learning environments be designed for media design education?* In the text below, we will discuss these insights on the basis of the three core features of situated learning introduced above: *communities of practice, participation,* and *authentic context.*

Community of practice

Students require access to real-world media design practices to learn the patterns of behavior of a media design studio. In turn, this access relies on the presence of appropriate clients in the partner-network of a school (Wesselink et al., 2010). For instance, our results reveal that understanding typical behavior associated with the pitching of concepts within the domain of media design, leads to more confidence in students when engaging with the studio environment and with clients.

Our case study results also suggest that the patterns of behavior surrounding feedback (e.g., how it is received and ought to be processed) may be among the most crucial patterns for novices to learn as they become a member of a community of practice. It requires feedback to understand one's own performance and which improvements need to be made to become an expert. Quality feedback seems particularly important to learn in order to communicate effectively and to develop a 'thick skin', which are both vital for a career in media design (Evans, 2020; McDonald, 2020). For instance, the discomfort experienced by studio members (of *Monstera*, see above) in providing their fellow members with critical feedback was followed by observing that the team as a whole improved as a result of it.

Furthermore, our case study reveals that the *quality of access* to the community of practice depends on the willingness of both partners (clients) as well as students to be transparent about their way of working, as was demonstrated by the client that stepped out of its role to make some tacit knowledge about industry expectations more explicit, and by the quotes from the self-reflection forms (of members of *Monstera*) that demonstrated a growing appreciation for honest criticism from fellow students.

Participation

Our case study results show that students familiarize themselves with the real-life complexity of media design practices through participation in the situated learning environment in the form of activities such as budgeting, pitching and communication. This complexity is nearly impossible to exhaustively describe or break down into facts and, therefore, to explain in the absence of actual participation.

The challenge for educators is to offer timely and relevant instruction. Although it is an ongoing debate whether or not scaffolding should be offered in situated learning environments at all (Roach et al., 2018), our case study seems to indicate that students *can* benefit from it, at least when the tasks that come with a certain role are unfamiliar to them. Through the use of studio logs and evaluation instruments, tutors can gain insight into the challenges that students encounter and reflect on those challenges where and when needed. It is important to note that our results also show that successful scaffolding depends on the quality of reflection throughout the situated learning experience: participants should be able to indicate their need for scaffolding in time. This requires both students and partners (clients) to be transparent about their way of working—it was also deemed important to learn the patterns of behavior of a community.

Finally, our case study shows the importance of the exploration of diverse roles within a media design studio. While only studio *Red Duke* chose to keep the designation of roles fluid on purpose, members of studios that started with strict divisions of roles (like *Cosmosfox*) often ended up exchanging roles between members later on in the simulation nevertheless. Our results suggest that the fluidity of roles relate to a sense of group identity. While this sense was arguably already present in *Red Duke* from the start, the growing willingness to assist fellow members in different roles reported in the self-reflection forms of members of *Cosmosfox* suggests they gradually developed such an identity.

Authentic Context

Although *Project Soho* intends to provide for an authentic context, our case study shows an important drawback of designing situated

81

learning environments inside schools: a school context is by default *un*authentic. The reluctance of students to provide other studio members with honest feedback, for instance, arguably stems from considering them more as fellow classmates rather than as professional colleagues. Also, detailed logs and frequent self-evaluation are arguably more common to a school context than to a professional media design studio. Furthermore, the logs suggest that clients generally addressed studio members as people who are still learning, rather than professional peers, as was indicated by the client that "broke character" to teach students about industry expectations regarding studio-client communication. Such behavior might not be authentic to the community of practice, but can be valuable to the situated learning experience.

An alternative view on the authenticity of a school context is that the school environment is *itself* a community of practice—a community that, more often than not, involves practicing professionals, albeit in the role of tutors, as well as one that provides for a safe learning environment, allowing students to make mistakes and speak openly about their learning processes and experiences. Although this suggests that some corruption of the authenticity of a situated learning experience by typical school behavior may have a positive impact on the learning experience, this effect depends on the quality of feedback from fellow students and partners.

CONCLUSIONS

Based on the discussion of our case study results, we draw three conclusions. First, situated learning environments for media design education should be designed so students can learn the patterns of behavior of a community of practice. This requires access to the community as well as transparency between partners and students, which seems particularly vital to learn media design soft skills. Second, participation in the situated learning environment is required to be able to learn from it. In media design education, such participation should be diverse, and is preferably combined with scaffolding. Third, the school context challenges the authenticity of situated learning environments, although patterns of behavior that belong to this school context can simultaneously be productive to the learning experience.

From these conclusions, three recommendations can be distilled that answer our research question: *How should situated learning environments be designed for media design education?* These three recommendations for the design of situated learning environments in media design education are:

1) foster the access to communities of practice, but also the quality of such access through transparency in the behavior of both students and partners;

2) facilitate learning through participation in the community of practice that is fluid in roles and supported by scaffolding; and

3) allow for patterns of behavior that belong to a school context to occur, even when these (temporarily) corrupt the authenticity of the learning environment.

Finally, we illustrate how these recommendations can be implemented with the three examples of improvements that we plan to make to future iterations of *Project Soho*. We will:

1) involve *Project Soho*-alumni that are now professionally active in the media design industry to provide scaffolding based on their personal experiences, combined with the needs felt by studio members at certain times in certain roles,

2) explain the benefits to students of allowing for fluidity in roles before they set up their studio agreement; and

3) brief clients more carefully on the pedagogical aspects of *Project Soho* to foster authentic experiences that simultaneously make for a safe learning environment.

82

REFERENCES

Barrett, T. & Moore, S. (Eds.). (2010). *New approaches to problem-based learning. Revitalizing your practice in higher education*. Routledge.

Choi, J. & Hannafin, M. (1995). Situated cognition and learning environments: Roles, structures, and implications for design. *Educational Technology Research & Development* 43, 53–69. https://doi.org/10.1007/BF02300472

DiSchiavi, E. (2019, July 12). *Applying theory to practice. Using technology to support situated cognition in education*. Technology and the Curriculum: Summer 2019. https://techandcurr2019.pressbooks.com/chapter/situated-cognition-meaningful-learning-space/

Donaldson, J & Barany, A. (2019). Designerly Ways of Learning. *Proceedings FabLearn* 2019 Eighth Annual Conference (50–56). https://doi.org/10.1145/3311890.3311897

Evans, J. (2020, March 21). *Vital Soft Skills Every Successful Animator Needs To Have*. Animatedjobs.com. https://animatedjobs.com/animationjobs/vital-soft-skills-every-successful-animator-needs-to-have/

Garson, G. & Khosrowpour, M. (2007). *Handbook of Research on Public Information Technology*. Information Science Reference.

Griffiths, T. & Guile, D. (2003). A Connective Model of Learning: The Implications for Work Process Knowledge. *European Educational Research Journal*. 2(1). 56-73. https://doi.org/10.2304/eerj.2003.2.1.10

Herrington, J. (2015). Introduction to Authentic Learning. In V. Bozalek, D. Ng'ambi, D. Wood, J. Herrington, J. Hardman, & A. Amory (Eds.), *Authentic learning, emerging technologies: Towards a transformative higher education pedagogy* (61–67). Routledge.

Herrington, J., & Oliver, R. (2000). An instructional design framework for authentic learning environments. *Education Technology Research and Development*. 48. 23–48.

McDonald, A. (2020, Feb 17). *10 essential Soft Skills you need to get a job in film, games and design industries*. The Rookies. https://discover.therookies.co/2020/02/17/10-essential-soft-skills-you-need-to-get-a-job-in-film-games-and-design-industries/

Northern Illinois University Center for Innovative Teaching and Learning (NIU-CITL) (2012). *Situated learning*. Instructional guide for university faculty and teaching assistants. https://www.niu.edu/citl/resources/guides/instructional-guide

Oregon Technology in Education Council (OTEC). (n.d.). *Learning Theories and Transfer of Learning*. https://otec.uoregon.edu/learning_theory.htm#Situated%20Learning

Kafai, Y. B. (2006). Playing and making games for learning: Instructionist and constructionist perspectives for game studies. *Games and Culture*. 1(1). 36-40. https://doi.org/10.1177/1555412005281767

Kaya, N., Aydin, S. & Durgut, S. (2016). Training Performance Evaluation Using the 360-Degree Feedback Method. *Proceedings 19th Eurasian Business and Economics Society*. 623-627. https://doi.org/10.13140/RG.2.1.3367.3843

Lave, J., & Wenger, E. (1991). *Learning in doing: Social, cognitive, and computational perspectives. Situated learning: Legitimate peripheral participation*. Cambridge University Press. https://doi.org/10.1017/CBO9780511815355

Lewis-Beck, M. S., Bryman, A., & Futing Liao, T. (2004). The SAGE *encyclopedia of social science research methods* (Vols. 1-0). Sage Publications, Inc. https://doi.org/10.4135/9781412950589

Roach, K., Tilley, A. & Mitchell, J. (2018). How authentic does authentic learning have to be?. *Higher Education Pedagogies*. 3(1), 495–509. https://doi.org/10.1080/23752696.2018.1462099

Shaltry, C., Henriksen, D., Lun Wu, M. & Dickson, P. (2013). Situated Learning with Online Portfolios, Classroom Websites and Facebook. *TechTrends*. 57(3). 20-25. https://doi.org/10.1007/s11528-013-0658-9

Simonsen, J., Svabo, C., Strandvad, S., Samson, K., Hertzum, M. & Hansen, O. (eds.). (2014). *Situated Design Methods*. MIT Press.

Stein, D. (1998). *Situated Learning in Adult Education*. ERIC Digest No. 195. 1-7. https://files.eric.ed.gov/fulltext/ED418250.pdf

Wärnestål, P. & Lindqvist, M. (2013). Designerly Ways of Teaching and Learning: A Course Structure for Interaction Design. *Journal for Higher Education*. 9(1), 179-188.

Wesselink, R., de Jong, C. & Biemans, H.J.A. (2010). Aspects of Competence-Based Education as Footholds to Improve the Connectivity Between Learning in School and in the Workplace. *Vocations and Learning* 3. 19–38. https://doi.org/10.1007/s12186-009-9027-4

Some Useful Information for Those in the Design Education Community Who Wish to Credibly Publish Their Research and Scholarship

MICHAEL GIBSON AND KEITH OWENS
The University of North Texas
Denton, Texas, USA

Keywords
Scholarly publishing, *Dialectic*, peer
review process, academic writing,
editing of scholarly prose, design
education

AN INTRODUCTION

This piece is informed by the experiential knowledge and understandings we've constructed as the production and editorial management team of the AIGA Design Educators' Community (DEC) scholarly journal *Dialectic*. Published by University of Michigan Publishing, *Dialectic* put out its first four issues between early 2017 and late 2019 before it was forced to temporarily interrupt its operations due to a disruption in its funding stream, and then the onset of the Covid-19 pandemic. Recently revived, *Dialectic* will publish its fifth issue in August or September of this year, followed by two issues per year beginning in 2022.

In our roles as journal co-editors, grant and conference submission reviewers, and as senior visual communication design faculty who have reviewed almost 80 design-rooted, university-level faculty candidates for tenure and promotion in the U.S., we have had many opportunities to critically read a diverse amalgam of scholarly writing, research reports, criticism, case studies, tenure dossiers and grant proposals. We are drawing from the knowledge and understandings we have cultivated from engaging in these experiences to inform what we will impart in this discussion. Additionally, we are also drawing from what we each have learned while engaging in our own efforts, singularly and collaboratively, focused on scholarly publishing, research reporting, and grant writing. As we deem it necessary and appropriate, we will also cite the work of others with significant scholarly publishing and editing experience in and around the design disciplines.

What is on offer here is not a formula or a set of algorithms that, if followed exactly and in sequence, is guaranteed to ensure the publication of your work in well-respected, peer-reviewed scholarly venues. It is rather intended as a set of guidelines that will hopefully prove to be—more-or-less—equal parts practically useful and constructive for those newly facing the challenges inherent in attempting to publish their research and scholarship in and around design education in reputable publications, as well as those who have accrued at least some experience doing this, but who are hoping to broaden their knowledge of and about these processes.

A Brief Presentation of What to AVOID If You Wish to Publish Your Design-Based Scholarship or Research in a Reputable, Peer-Reviewed Journal

We are not alone as journal editors and producers working in and around design (not to mention a myriad of other disciplines) who repeatedly receive passionately worded, zealously recounted descriptions of some instance of what the author purports to be a novel teaching approach, methodology or method,[1] or the outcomes

---

1 We have read much as editors and grant and tenure reviewers that suggests many designers and design educators, at least in the U.S., don't learn the difference between the terms "methodology" and "method." This also means they often don't conceive of methods as means to achieve a given end or accomplish a particular goal, nor do they learn to think of methodologies as a system of methods that can be employed to affect a specific activity, type of work or study, or type of project. People who work in academia and the private sector whose bases of knowledge and understandings are informed by what they have

of planning and operating these. These pieces tend to be supported by examples of student work, or documentation of a participatory project that involved a population or a community "in need," or both. Simply put, these kinds of pieces can be described as, "I developed and operated a process that seemed cool to me, and then to my students and our collaborators, and then it actually turned out to be *really* cool, and the students learned a great deal and our collaborators were really happy with the outcome(s). The end."

We have also had occasion to review a plethora of research papers and project summaries over the past couple of decades that are similarly flawed: they articulate what was developed, formulated, and performed to yield results from a single project, event or operation, often with a relatively small and narrowly constituted n-group. They are written as if almost no one else has ever thought to engage in this type of research before, so no (or very little) mention is made in the writing of where the endeavor is located or situated in the canon, or "landscape," of other research that has been conducted in or around this area previously. These pieces are presented as one-offs—"I engaged in this singularly focused, research project and here are the results"—without any, or often not nearly enough, *contextualization*. Failing

to effectively reference the work of others who have engaged in work similar to what is on offer in a given submission tends to indicate that the submission's author(s) are also failing to provide evidence to support whatever approaches, rationales, and processes are being described in the writing.[2] Additionally, failing to effectively reference the work of others who have engaged in research, practice or scholarship that could inform and contextualize the contents of a given submission tends to cause most reviewers to recommend against publication or funding.

With regard to both of the problematic types of writing described above, the lack of effective contextualization usually means that some crucial questions that should have been defined and addressed prior to attempting either the novel teaching approach, methodology or method, or the research project, were ignored or simply not even conceived or considered. These include the following, stated somewhat broadly to encompass a wide variety of situations.

> » Was the teaching innovation or research project informed by a specific, extant approach and methodology, and if so (hopefully—yes...), which one(s) and why?
>
> » What were or are the objectives and goals (not the same things) of the teaching innovation or research project?
>
> » What suppositions or hypotheses were tested during the operation of the teaching innovation or the research project, and why these in particular?
>
> » What methods guided the progress of whatever was operationalized, and why were these utilized?
>
> » What data was yielded, and what did the authors' analysis of this data reveal?
>
> » What evidence has your engagement in these endeavors produced that could be

---

learned as (for example) social scientists, programmers, business managers, and engineers tend to be taught to think of a methodology as being akin to a toolbox that is carried into a particular type of situation, and a method as a tool that exists in that toolbox. So—as was explained to one of the authors of this piece by a psychologist when both were in graduate school 30 years ago—"just as someone looking to fix a leaky pipe would take a plumber's toolbox into that situation, and then have access to tools within it like pipe wrenches, channel lock pliers and plungers, someone looking to better understand why select individuals are scared to fly on airplanes would operate a phenomenological methodology to guide information gathering methods such as one-on-one interviews, online-facilitated surveys and interviews with groups of two or three people." (Phenomenological methodologies have gained increased popularity over the past decade or so among user experience designers, who often must inform their design decision-making with understandings about how and why individuals respond and behave as they do as they attempt to complete tasks and engage in given transactions or experiences.)

It has been the authors' experience over the last quarter century that lacking knowledge of and about how to employ given methodologies and the methods associated with them to affect design processes is less prevalent in areas such as user experience and interaction design, industrial design, and architecture. With that stated, addressing how to more effectively confront this problem across other disciplinary areas of design, such as in visual communication design/graphic design, will have to be the topic of another article (as it already has been addressed by many writing under the aegis of many other disciplines).

---

2 Gertrude Himmelfarb wrote a piece on using footnotes and referencing that was published in the New York Times Book Review in 1991 that is as useful to authors attempting to publish scholarly work now as it was 30 years ago. It can be found at: http://msa.maryland.gov/ecp/10/214/html/0003.html. Another useful and downright-fun-to-read resource on footnoting and referencing is Anthony Grafton's book *"The Footnote: A Curious History" (Harvard University Press, 1999), which has become required reading at the undergraduate level in many disciplines of study operating in American universities (unfortunately, design does not tend to be among these).*

used to support one or more rationales to improve design education to guide future design decision-making?

> » Is the research project or teaching innovation generalizable (that is: applicable or adaptable to other contexts or situations) in some way, and, if so, why, or, if not, why not?

What Occurs During the Early Phases of the Review Process, and Why These Are So Crucial for Would-Be Authors to Understand

Every submission for possible publication that *Dialectic* receives undergoes a rigorously facilitated, critical review process that is fairly standard across academic and professional disciplines as diverse as engineering, economics, chemistry, and philosophy. This process begins with a desk review, which begins with one to three members of an editorial team engaging in a preliminary read of whatever has been submitted to ensure that it meets what we refer to as our *logistical criteria:*[3] word counts must be adhered to ("not too many, not too few…"), the document itself must be formatted according to the publication's specifications, and the piece must be written according to the guidelines specified in the Chicago Manual of Style. (Specific journals and periodicals require most of their prose to be written according to a particular style manual, such as APA/the American Psychological Association, MLA/the Modern Language Association, or CMS/the Chicago Manual of Style.) Once it has been determined that our logistical criteria have been met, an assessment of the organizational structure of the piece is coupled with an evaluation of its phrase-to-phrase, sentence-to-sentence, and paragraph-to-paragraph writing style. This is the phase of our editorial process during which roughly half of the submissions *Dialectic* receives are removed from consideration for publication. What follows is an articulation of the most common reasons submissions are rejected during the desk review process.

> » The phrase-to-phrase, sentence-to-sentence, and paragraph-to-paragraph use of prose in the piece are flawed grammatically or syntactically, or otherwise inhibit the

effective readability of the piece (this is, unfortunately, an incredibly common problem—we have received a large volume of submissions that make it apparent that those who wrote them are unfamiliar with the simple-but-effective instructions for clear and concise writing articulated in Strunk & White's easy-to-read-and-utilize book *"Elements of Style,"* or the somewhat more in-depth book *"Stylish Academic Writing"* by Helen Sword)

> » The authors don't clearly state a thesis or essential argument/raison d'etre at the outset of their piece, which entails a clear articulation of not only "what the piece is about," but *why* it would be worth a reader's precious time and energy to read its contents

> » (as has already been addressed) Authors fail to situate how what they're offering/ writing about "fits into and differs from" the larger context of scholarship that's already been created around the examination of the topic(s) of their piece

> » The authors make key claims in the piece that are unsupported by evidence or well-argued rationales

> » The essential argumentative structure of the piece is poorly constructed and organized

> » The authors fail to clearly articulate meaningful or viable conclusions, or effectively crafted summations, or specifically contextualized and articulated calls for further types of research, at the culminations of their submissions (in articles that exist to credibly report out the results of a given research endeavor or approach, calling for other researchers to expand on the authors' research, or to conduct additional research to either corroborate or refute what the authors reported, often provides readers with "starting points" to initiate research that will contribute to the bases of knowledge and understandings that inform a given discipline or disciplinary area)

> » The authors delve into details, or get "sidetracked," in one or more areas of their narrative in ways that obfuscate their central theme or main message

86

---

3 *Dialectic's* submission parameters can be read by visiting the material located at: https://quod.lib.umich.edu/d/dialectic/submit

» The piece has been written in a manner that assumes the reader possesses extant knowledge of whatever is being articulated or explained, so much so that crucial explanatory or contextually relevant information is left out

» The authors use unnecessary or inappropriate jargon, or use purposefully obscure or difficult language, in an attempt to make their submission seem rigorous or serious

Only after a submission has been assessed to be "worthy of further evaluation" during the desk review process does it advance to the next phase, during which it is read and analyzed more deeply by between two and four peer reviewers who have expertise in the subject matter that constitutes the submission. It is these reviewers who offer more probative critical commentary—in writing—to the authors of the submission so that they may execute whatever revisions, omissions and augmentations that are called for to ensure that it can eventually be published. Once these final alterations have been made, it is up to the managing editors of a given journal to decide whether to publish it (if, at this point, the piece is assessed to still need extensive re-writing, many journals will reject it, as they cannot afford to incur the time delay or the expense that re-writing may require at this juncture in the process).

TWO "BIG, BUT NOT-SO-SECRET IDEAS" THAT CAN HELP YOU SUCCEED IN YOUR SCHOLARLY PUBLICATION ATTEMPTS

One of the premier obstacles that would-be authors of the wide variety of scholarship and research that a journal like *Dialectic* must confront is that so many of them made it all the way through graduate school without being challenged to engage in the cyclic process of developing, writing, receiving initial feedback about, re-writing, and then receiving final assessments of their scholarly, or academic, prose. This is still an egregious shortcoming inherent in far too many master's level curricula across the design disciplines in the U.S. (where it is too often assumed that graduate students will somehow magically learn to craft effective academic writing when they reach either the doctoral level of study, or they begin to fulfill teaching or design leadership careers). The

need for more American graduate level design programs to immerse students in learning experiences that challenge them to "write better" is a topic that requires a more broadly informed and deeply probative inquiry than can be articulated in this discourse. What is on offer in this, the closing section of this piece, is a brief diatribe on the negative ramifications of this set of circumstances, along with a means to enact two ideas that have the potential to positively alter the negative effects of this.

The key concept to understand here is the effect that this shortcoming has had, and continues to have, on how design education is facilitated in many graduate and undergraduate programs in the U.S. It has resulted in a large number of people embarking on careers in design education, management, or thought leadership who are ill-equipped to effectively meet one of the primary challenges endemic to all of these career and life paths. They all require knowing how to structure and support essential arguments and rationales with evidence articulated in effectively communicative prose, as well as how to clearly express why particular types of data analyses were used to affect specific design decisions, and, ultimately, knowing how to convey these in text that is consistently engaging. Doing these things well helps ensure that what a given design educator, manager, or thought leader has done can be validated in some way as attempts are made to build upon whatever initiatives they have formulated and operated. It also helps ensure that the outcomes of various types of design strategies and decision-making can be effectively assessed by means other than someone's intuitively rooted assertion that whatever was undertaken worked well (or failed to). Not being able to craft effectively communicative scholarly writing restricts too many critical conversations about design and its affects (on social, technological, environmental, economic and public policy change) to being constrained within the realm of the how, rather than expanding into the realm of the why. It also often prevents designers from being able to collaborate effectively with others from outside our discipline who possess the abilities and cores of knowledge necessary to do this well, and who are accustomed to having to express the significance of and provide validation for their work by means of writing well and then publishing what they have written.

One of the central reasons offered in the previous section regarding why articles often fail to advance

87

beyond the desk review phase of the assessment process of *Dialectic* and other scholarly journals was that they are judged to not be worth a reader's precious time and attention to read. They may also be rejected because they are assessed as not making a significant enough contribution of new knowledge and understanding to the discipline within which a given journal is embedded (for example, design, and the research, scholarship and educational endeavors that support it). A way to help ensure that both of these objectives are effectively met—at least from perspective of *Dialectic's* producers and editors—is for the would-be authors of and about[4] design research and scholarship to work with an experienced, independent editor[5] of scholarly prose from the earliest stages of their writing development processes.

Specifically, one of the things we have learned in working with *Dialectic's* would-be authors is that involving an experienced editor when a project is still in the abstract-to-rough-draft stage can help both novice and experienced authors avoid many of the pitfalls described in the two sets of bullet points that occur earlier in this piece. Effective editors will ask well-framed, broadly informed, deeply probative questions about why you have chosen to write about what you have, why you have chosen to operate whatever viewpoints, or editorial stances, you have, why you have chosen to structure your piece as you have, and why what you are writing about should be worth your intended readership's precious time. Effective editors of the type of prose that *Dialectic* and other scholarly journals publish charge reasonable rates per hour (or per the number of words they have to assess), and what you will spend to gain their wise counsel early on will more than make up for what you risk losing with a rejection or a sizable re-writing task that could have been avoided if it has been attended to earlier in the process.

Finally, one of the aspects of co-producing and co-managing *Dialectic* that has surprised us the most is, frankly, how taken aback or otherwise put off so many would-be authors from the realm of design and design education are when they are informed that their work has been deemed unacceptable for publication based on the criteria described earlier in this piece. Many have reacted with a kind of insulted incredulity when informed that their research approach does not effectively account for or locate itself within other similar research endeavors that have preceded it, or that their line-by-line prose is not suitable for scholarly publication, or that what may be incredibly important scholarship in their personal estimation has not been deemed all that important to our readership according to whatever group of peer reviewers assessed their submission. Our sense of why those who have been taken aback by *Dialectic's* rejection of their work is, more than any other single factor, attributable to something that I first heard voiced by a now-former, design-based, scholarly journal editor more than 25 years ago at an academic conference hosted by the University of Alberta in Edmonton, Canada: "Far too many designers and design educators don't read critically, don't know how to read critically, and aren't particularly interested in reading critically."

This editor's blunt words weren't so much a condemnation of designers and design educators not reading the scholarly journals that informed our discipline, but, in his/her/their experience, not knowing how to read (or wanting to read) in ways that ensured the reading experience itself played an actual role in not only the discovery of new knowledge, but in the construction of it, the latter of which tends to require broadly informed critical thinking, and a willingness to question information presented as facts. It was, and still is, the kind of reading that tends to be abetted by the use of (in the days before smartphones and iPads) highlighter markers and cheap-but-effective red, ball-point pens for identifying what the reader believed to be essential information embedded in the text (encountered in those days only on paper), and then expounding on it in his, her or their words. It is the kind of reading that helps build and sustain contextual understandings, and that fuels curiosity, and that prizes questions over answers, and that, over time, aids and abets strong scholarly writing. Bottom line: if you desire to have your scholarship and research published in a well-reputed

---

4   These are not the same thing. Briefly: knowing and understanding of something is derived from personally doing or experiencing it directly, and is difficult to transfer or express (examples include riding a bicycle and playing the guitar; this satisfies many people's definitions for tacit knowledge). Knowing and understanding about something is easy to record and share in ways that can eventually be applied by others as they, for example, transition from one job or work duty to another (this satisfies many people's definitions of explicit and implicit knowledge).

5   In this context, an "independent editor" is someone who is not associated with the journal within which a given authors is trying to publish his, her or their work.

academic venue, it's an exceptionally good idea to be in the habit of regularly and critically reading the published scholarship and research of others working in and around your discipline. As you do this, and especially if you do this with regularity (try setting aside three to four quiet hours per week for this, at minimum) ideas for initiating your own research, scholarship or critical inquiry may begin to "spark and swirl" as a result of your engaging in this more critically engaged reading process. You'll also be equipping yourself with a much more diversely populated and robustly supported amalgam of knowledge and understandings with which to guide not just your writing endeavors, but your approaches to engaging in design processes, and to teaching them.

Vissual Essays

SHIFT

→

92 TYPE Portrait

YEOHYUN AHN

TYPE Portrait

YEOHYUN AHN

Assistant Professor of Graphic Design
and Interaction Design

Graphic Design Program,
Art Department,
University of Wisconsin Madison

Keywords
typography, visual expression, selfie,
generative photography, self-portrait,
generative art

ABSTRACT

Typography is regarded as a form of art to make written language expressive. TYPE Portrait is a series of generative typography as self-portrait photographs by the designer. It portrays her sense of invisibility as a woman of color and as an academic stranger in professional areas of American society. The designer started taking her generative selfie in 2015 to raise awareness of Asian female faculty being isolated and marginalized in predominantly white institutions of US campuses. The computational processes expand the concepts of traditional self-portraits to generative selfies delivering specific thoughts or feelings. Based on the type choices, different emotions and moods can visually be provided through generative selfies. TYPE Portrait uses diverse typefaces to convey feelings and thoughts in the generative selfie. It shows possibilities to use each typeface's personality to be expressive and visually appealing through generative typography.

INTRODUCTION

A selfie is a photograph typically taken of oneself with a smartphone or webcam and shared through social media. Today, over 1 million selfies are taken every day. Selfies are not always as spontaneous as they seem. A selfie is a form of art. It can be a purposeful communication tool. TYPE Portrait is an extension of Selfie + CODE, a generative selfie collection by the designer. Computational processes expand the concepts of traditional self-portraits to computational visual languages conveying specific thoughts or feelings. The designer started taking generative selfies in 2015 to raise awareness of Asian female faculty isolated in a predominantly white institution. These generative selfies capture psychological moments to express individual identities devalued by a homogeneous institution in the US. These were shared through social media. Using social media networks like Facebook as a virtual support system, the artist was enabled to persist and survive in a regionally isolated and exclusive community. It has eventually brought her psychological reconciliation and healing to succeed in dealing with difficulties. The project extended to include the medium of typography, with the title TYPE Portrait. Each typeface has a visual personality. TYPE Portrait is visual research using diverse typefaces to embed visual expressions and emotions into generative selfies.

BACKGROUND

The population of Asian female faculty members is small but growing in higher education in the United States. This group may struggle to navigate between two exclusive communities: Asian and American. Asian cultures predominately conceive being a professor as a male position. It is a socially privileged and highly respected position in patriarchal Asian cultures. Asian female faculty occasionally encounter circumstances less inclusive and invisibly exclusive in Asian communities. The emerging population of Asian female faculty members may threaten the well-established patriarchal hierarchy controlled and led by men in these Asian communities. Asian communities predominately pressure Asian women to perform the traditional roles of mothers and homemakers. Asian female faculty bonded with these cultures are inevitably destined to be isolated and

92

marginalized by their ethnic groups to avoid criticism toward their nontraditional roles. Additionally, Asian female faculty members suffer from stereotypes, including being perceived as uncomplaining to authority, when working for predominately white institutions. The classroom may be a minefield of student resistance and negative attitudes (Nguyen, 2016). According to the paper, "Women of Color Faculty at the University of Michigan: Recruitment, Retention, and Campus Climate," women faculty of color might be the most marginalized faculty on US campuses. Challenges include isolation, high attrition, student evaluations, peer perception, more service responsibilities (Cox, 2008).

SELFIE + CODE

Generative selfies taken by the designer since 2015 have formed a collection called Selfie + CODE. This project has captured psychological moments to express individual identities devalued and deconstructed by homogeneous institutions and ethnocentric groups in the US [Fig. 1].

Figure 1: Selfie + CODE I

The visual style of the project was inspired by two art movements from the 19th-century. The first is Impressionism that involves capturing a moment, such as Claude Monet's *Sunrise*. The second is Expressionism that expresses inner troubles and feelings of anxiety, such as Edward Munch's *The Scream* [Fig. 2].

This project references Mirror Library by Daniel Shiffman in Processing. Mirror Library transforms each pixel from a real-time video source into a rectangle on brightness levels captured by an internal web camera. Each shape is changed into a line to draw the moments reflecting the visual theme, being ignored, brushed off, refused, as an Asian female faculty on US campuses. Further, several custom variables, functions, and color palettes are added to express the visual theme [Fig. 3].

93

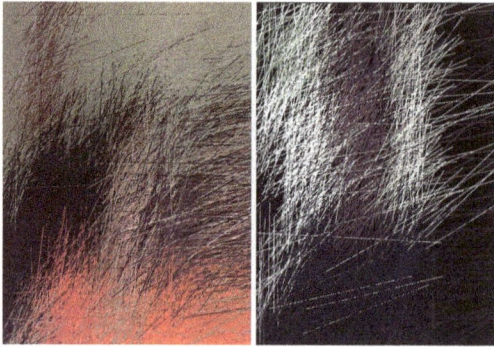

Figure 3: Initial sketches by the Being Ignored 1.0

The selfie series was taken in the author's office space in a regionally isolated predominantly white institution to represent the creation of a space for Asian female faculty on US campuses. The office light was intentionally controlled to be darker to express the moments being brushed off and rejected on US campuses. An internal web camera captured the author's self-portrait photographs using the computer algorithm, Being Ignored 1.0, and eliminated facial expressions to convey the sense of being treated as less valued, unremarkable, and unworthy of attention. The photographs were taken at different angles and with different light levels repeatedly and sequentially. The process was similar to professional photos being taken in a photo studio [Fig. 4].

Figure 4: Selfie + CODE II, Final Outputs

TYPE PORTRAIT

Typography is an art form where the text is expressive and highly visual. Selfie-taking is self-expression to convey a mood or share a story through social media. Common facial expressions use a wide range of emotions through a selfie. Each typeface has a personality reflecting specific visual atmospheres and moods. The entire alphabet set from A to Z is applied to Selfie + CODE to transform each line into each letter using the text() and string () function in Mirror Library in Processing. Additionally, essential visual elements such as circles and lines are added to enhance the typography composition. This visual research uses typefaces embedded within selfies given that facial expressions are used to convey feelings and thoughts. The designer chose to integrate the following typefaces with selfies to investigate how the two could come together to be expressive and visual.

The following typefaces were chosen to embed themselves into selfies to investigate how selfies integrate with typefaces to be expressive and visual.

HELVETICA

Helvetica is a modern, intelligent, and stylish typeface designed by Max Miedinger in 1957. It is among the most widely used sans-serif typefaces [Fig. 5].

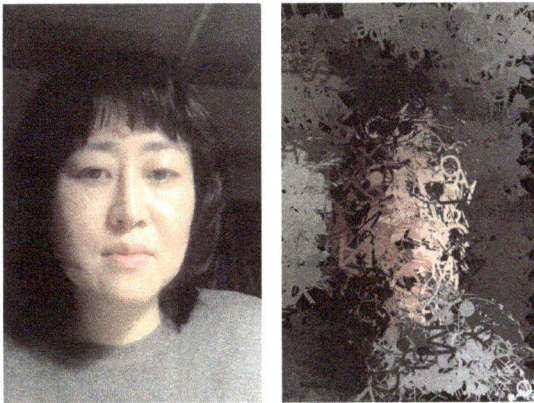

Figure 5: Left: Initial Selfie, Right: Generative selfie with the Helvetica typeface using an English alphabet from A to Z.

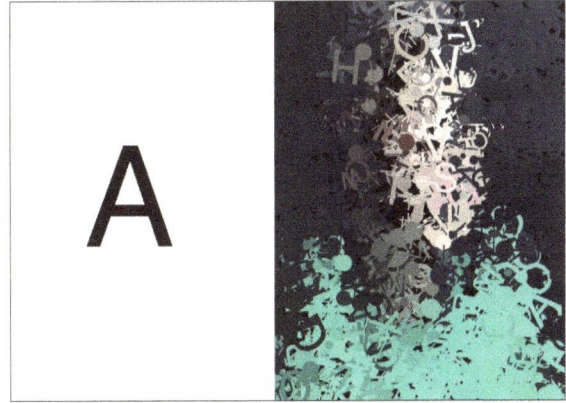

Figure 6: Left: Helvetica A, Right: Generative selfie with the Helvetica typeface

Figure 6-2: Typographic Selfie + CODE: Helvetica Series

95

TIMES NEW ROMAN

Times New Roman is an intellectual, confident, academic, and professional typeface designed by Stanley Morison Victor Lardent in 1931. The British newspaper, *The Times*, commissioned it. This typeface is one of the most popular and influential typefaces in history [Fig. 7].

Figure 7: Times A, Right: Generative selfie with the Times typeface Left

FUTURA

Futura is a modern, practical, comfortable, and capable sans-serif typeface designed by Paul Renner in 1927 (Hyndman, 2016) [Fig. 8].

Figure 8: Left: Futura A, Right: Generative selfie with the Futura typeface

DIDOT

Didot is a sophisticated, polished, and professional typeface developed from 1784–1811 by the Didot family [Fig. 9].

Figure 9: Left: Didot A, Right: Generative selfie with the Didot typeface

BASKERVILLE

Baskerville is a traditional, credible, and neutral typeface designed by John Baskerville in the 1750s. It remains prevalent in publication designs [3] [Fig 10].

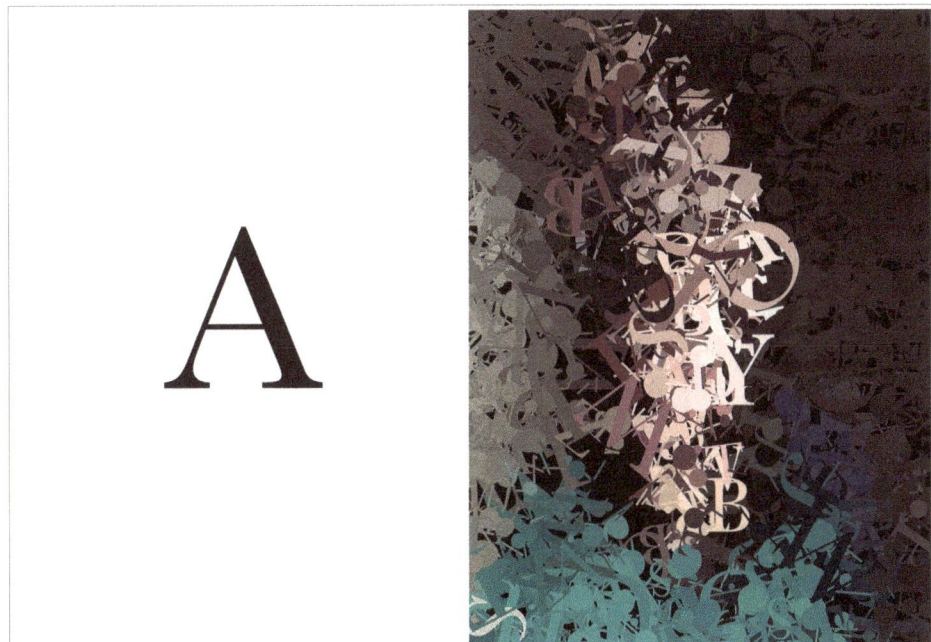

Figure 10: Left: Baskerville A, Right: Generative selfie with the Baskerville typeface

ZAPFINO

Zapfino is a calligraphic typeface designed for the Linotype machine by typeface designer Hermann Zapf in 1998.

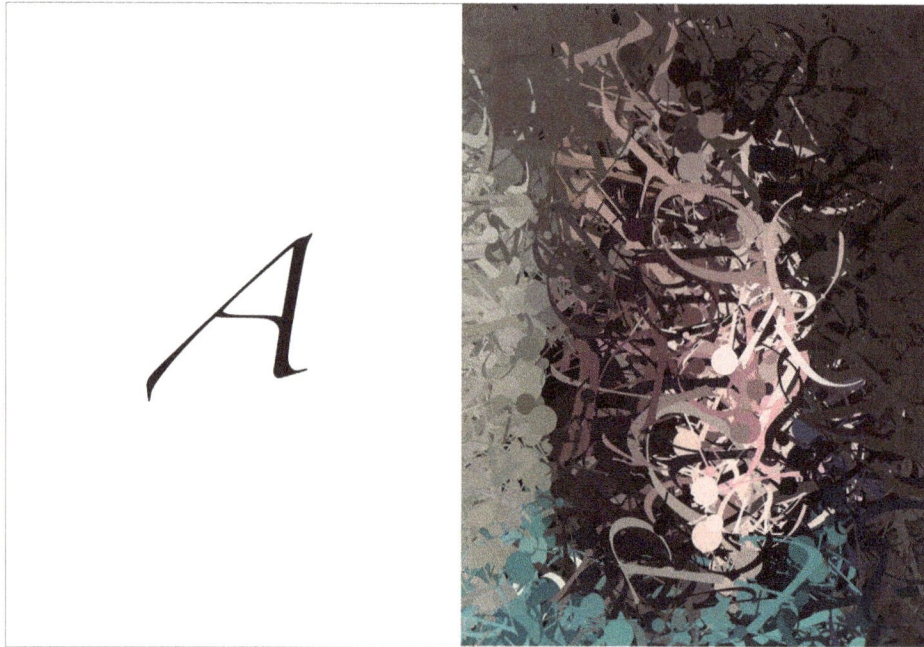

Figure 11: Left: Zapfino A, Right: Generative selfie with the Zapfino typeface

ASMELINA HARLEY

Asmelina Harley is an elegant calligraphy script typeface. Arif Dwi designed this typeface at the Kotak Kuning Studio in 2019 [Fig. 12].

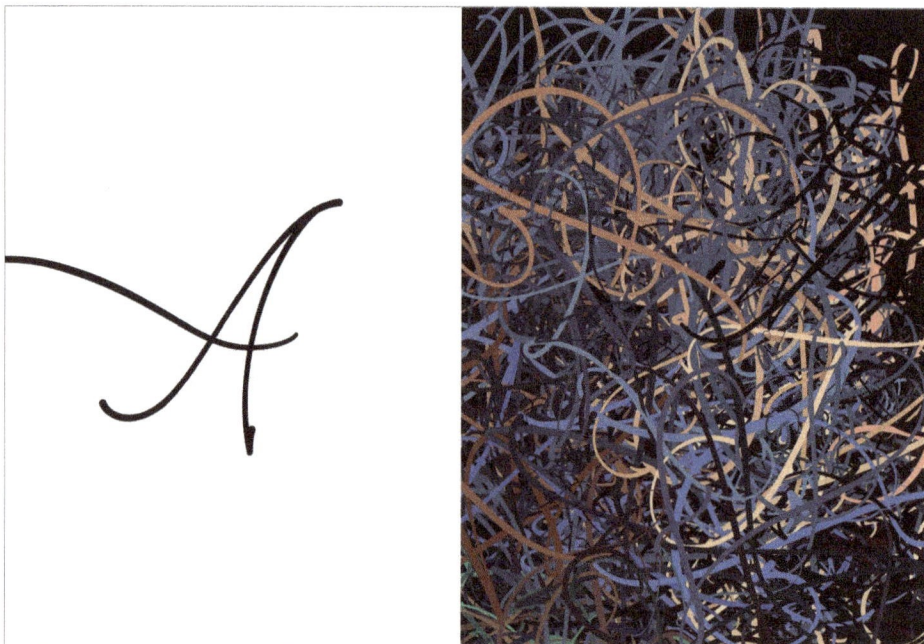

Figure 12 Left: Asmelina Harley A, Right: Generative Selfie with the typeface, Asmelina Harley

Figure 13: Generative selfie with the Asmelina Harley typeface

KOREAN TYPEFACE: NANUM MEYONGJO AND NAUM GOTHIC

These use two Korean typefaces, Namun Gothic is similar to the san-serif typeface, and Namun Meyongjo is similar to Serif typeface. Sandoll Communication and Fontrix designed these typefaces in South Korea [Fig 14].

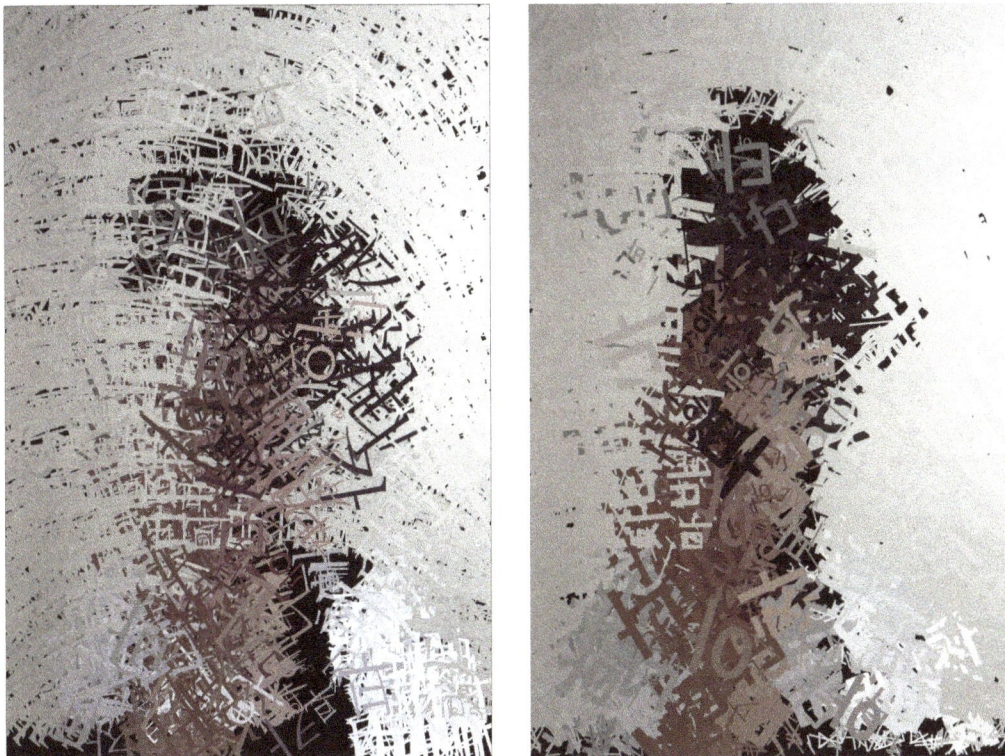

Figure 14: Left: Generative selfie with the Namun Meyongjo typeface, Right: Generative selfie with the Namun Gothic typeface

99

5.9 HANGUL ALPHABET

The Hangul Alphabet employs an intercultural typography method. It uses a custom English typeface, Hangul, inspired by Korean vowels and constants, to construct an English alphabet set from A to Z, designed by Taekyoem Lee. The Hangul typeface is legible for English readers but not legible and readable in Korean since it is an English typeface, not a Korean typeface.

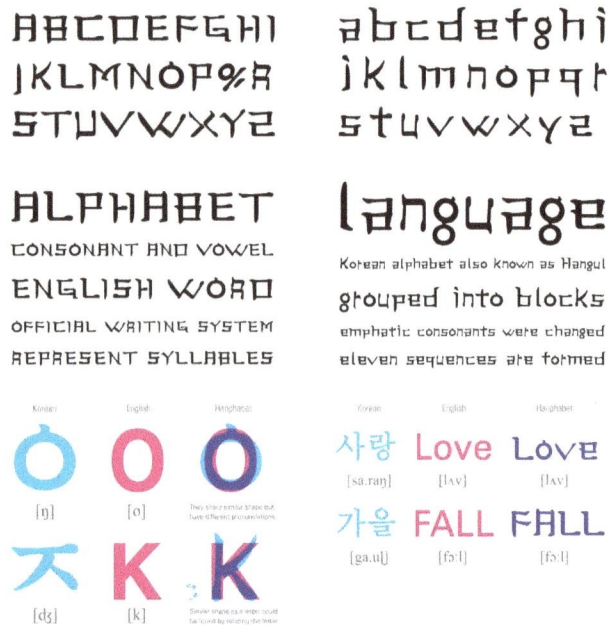

Figure 15: Left: Hangul Alphabet by Taekyoem Lee, Right: Generative selfie with the Hangul Alphabet typeface

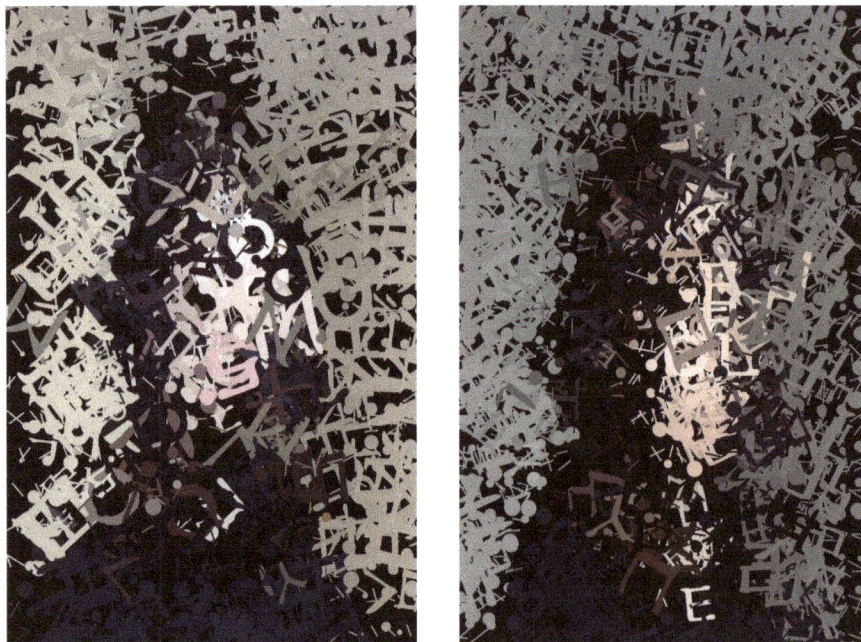

Figure 16: Generative selfies with the Hangul Alphabet typeface

CONCLUSION

This research shows how to use the typefaces and generative selfies to convey feelings and thoughts. It has extended typographic practices and applications. The study demonstrates how traditional typography principles and procedures, including typeface choice and arrangement and visual expression, would be applicable and workable to generative selfies made with creative coding. It shows possibilities to use each typeface's personality to be expressive and visually appealing in generative design and art. Future research will involve more diverse non-western typefaces and experimental custom typefaces, and generative selfies. The designer will provide future workshop opportunities for art and design communities to increase this project's visibility and enhance professional participation.

REFERENCES:

1. Nguyen, CF, 2016, Asian American Women Faculty: Stereotypes and Triumphs, University of San Francisco, San Francisco, CA, pp. 129 - 136.

2. Cox, A, 2008, Women of Color Faculty at the University of Michigan: Recruitment, Retention, and Campus Climate, University of Michigan, MI, pp. 2

3. Hyndman, S. (2016) Why Fonts Matter. GINGKO Press, CA, pp.80-81

PEER-REVIEWED INTERNATIONAL AND NATIONAL PRESENTATIONS

2021 "TYPE+CODE Series," Design and the Environment Session, C.A.A. (College Art Association Conference), N.Y.C., NY

2020 "Typographic Selfie + CODE," ATyfI (Association Typographique Internationale), Paris, France

2020 "Typographic Selfie + CODE," Valencia Design Education Forum, Valencia, Spain

2020 "Selfie + CODE," UDA Webinar, United Designs Alliance, Seoul, South Korea

2020 "Typographic Selfie + CODE I to IV," DEL (Digitally Engaged Learning) Conference, Parsons, N.Y.C., NY

2020 "Social Homelessness on U.S. Campuses," SIGGRAPH Diversity and Inclusion Summit, Washington DC, U.S.A.

2020 "TYPE + CODE VI & V," SEGD (Society of Experiential Graphic Design), Portland, Oregon, U.S.A.

2020 "Typographic Selfie + CODE," CICA New Media Art Conference, CICA Museum, Kimpo, South Korea

2019 "Social Homelessness on U.S. Campuses," IEEE GEM (Games Entertainment & Media), Yale University, New Haven,

2018 "Social Homelessness on U.S. campuses," Design Incubation Colloquium 5.1, DePaul University, Chicago, IL

SOLO EXHIBITIONS

2021 "TYPE PORTRAIT," Brooks Steven Gallery, Milwaukee Art Institute of Art & Design, Milwaukee, WI

2020 "Typographic Selfie + CODE," CICA New Media Art Conference, CICA Museum, Kimpo, South Korea

INVITED ARTIST TALKS

2021 Artist Talk, "TYPE PORTRAIT," Brooks Steven Gallery, Milwaukee Art Institute of Art & Design, Milwaukee, WI

2021 Guest Artist Talk, Workshop, Senior Portfolio Review and Juror for Student Annual Competition, Graphic Design Program, School of Art, Illinois State University, Normal, IL

PEER-REVIEWED ARTIST TALKS

2020 "Social Homelessness on U.S. Campuses," ISEA (International Symposium on Electronic Art), Montreal, CA

2016 "Being Ignored," ISEA (International Symposium on Electronic Arts), Hong Kong, China

PEER-REVIEWED RESEARCH PAPERS

2020 "Typographic Selfie + CODE," E.V.A. (International Electronic Visualisation & the Arts conferences), London, England

2019 "Social Homelessness on U.S. Campuses," IEEE GEM (Games Entertainment & Media), Yale University, New Haven, CT

2019 «Social Homelessness on U.S. Campuses,» ARTECH 2019: Digital Media Art Ecosystems, Braga, Portugal

PEER-REVIEWED INTERNATIONAL AND NATIONAL EXHIBITIONS

2021 "Typographic Selfie + CODE: Helvetica III", International Juried Exhibition, "Glitch", International Digital Media and Art's Conference, Winona State University, Winona, MN

2019 "Social Homelessness on U.S. Campuses," ARTECH 2019: Digital Media Art Ecosystems, Braga, Portugal

2017 "Being Ignored," Media Arts Nexus, NTU, Singapore

2017 "Being Ignored," Web3D 2017 Conference, Brisbane, Australia

2017 "Self Generative Ver 3.0," Digitalia," National Juried Exhibition for Digital Art, Barret Art Center, Poughkeepsie, New York

2016 "Self Generative Portrait Ver 2.2," International Digital Media and Arts' Annual Conference, Winona State University, Winona, MN

2016 "Code/Switch," Women Made Gallery, Chicago, IL

PUBLICATIONS

2021 "Typographic Selfie + CODE: Times New Roman," UDA Annual 2020", United Designs Alliance, Seoul, South Korea

2020 "Typographic Selfie + CODE," Into the Clouds: New Media Art 2021, CICA Press, Kimpo, South Korea

101

SHIFT

3–7 AUGUST 2020 ✳ VIRTUAL SUMMIT

AIGA DEC STEERING COMMITTEE